They Said It First

The Wisdom of the Ancient Greeks and Romans

Kenneth F. Kitchell, Jr.

Bolchazy-Carducci Publishers, Inc.
Mundelein, Illinois USA

Editor: Amelia Wallace

Design & Layout: Adam Phillip Velez

They Said It First
The Wisdom of the Ancient Greeks and Romans

Kenneth F. Kitchell, Jr.

Bolchazy-Carducci Publishers, Inc.
1570 Baskin Road
Mundelein, Illinois 60060
www.bolchazy.com

Printed in the United States of America
2019
by Publishers' Graphics

ISBN 978-0-86516-864-0

Library of Congress Cataloging-in-Publication Data

Names: Kitchell, Kenneth F., Jr., 1947- author.
Title: They said it first : the wisdom of the ancient Greeks and Romans /
    Kenneth F. Kitchell, Jr.
Description: Mundelein, Illinois, USA : Bolchazy-Carducci Publishers, Inc.,
    2019. | Includes bibliographical references and index. | An anthology of
    Greek and Latin quotations with English equivalents.
Identifiers: LCCN 2019007187 | ISBN 9780865168640 (pbk. : alk. paper)
Subjects: LCSH: Quotations, Greek. | Quotations, Latin.
Classification: LCC PN6080 .K53 2019 | DDC 808.88/2

For Roger

Servandus ergo est omni diligentia raro inventus amicus, est enim alter ego.

*—*Seneca, *De Moribus* 20.

Nullum'st iam dictum quod non dictum sit prius.

There is nothing that's been said now that hasn't been said before.

–Terence, *The Eunuch*, prologue 41.

Pereant qui ante nos nostra dixerunt.

May those who spoke our thoughts before we did perish.

–Aelius Donatus, cited by St. Jerome, *Commentary on Ecclesiastes*, ch. 1 (Migne 1.23.390).

Contents

Acknowledgements

The Roman playwright Plautus wrote many memorable lines, as the reader will soon see. One of my favorites is "Nil agit qui diffidentem verbis solatur suis; is est amicus, qui in dubia re iuvat, ubi re est opus" (One who comforts an anxious friend with his words does nothing; that one is a friend who helps in a tight spot when there is need of action; *Epid.* 111–12). I am indebted to countless friends who remain friends despite being pestered with questions as I put this collection together. The anonymous readers of the original manuscript greatly improved it through their careful reading and sage advice. To Bridget Dean and Don Sprague for their enthusiasm and support in the initial stages. And, finally, to Amelia Wallace, for her editorial patience, keen eye, and immense common sense. The flaws that undoubtedly remain began as and remain my own, but as the book reminds us, "Humanum errare est."

Introduction

Origins

This book came gradually to life from the office door of a newly appointed instructor at Louisiana State University. Being a new faculty member at one's first job is rather like finding yourself sitting at a formal dining table for the first time. Before you lie five forks, three spoons, four knives (are we going to be attacked?), four plates, and five different glasses. Fearing to appear gauche, a wise person does not eat a thing until he sees the person next to him reach for an implement.

So it is when one begins life as a teacher in higher education. What is the campus's norm for dress? How are you to be addressed and how should you address the students? And, of course, the ever vital question of what to do with one's office door. It became obvious quite early that there are basically two kinds of professors' doors. One sort keeps his or her door pristine, adorned only with a dignified name plate and, perhaps, an envelope to facilitate receiving or giving back student work. At the other end of the spectrum lies the door covered entirely with things that reflect the opinions of the office's resident— political cartoons, op-ed pieces, funny pictures, bible verses, pictures of cats, a map showing where the Dalai Lama is at any given time.

I opted for restraint, and apart from a sign giving my office hours, I confined myself to posting, once a week, a new quotation from antiquity, sometimes with a modern parallel. I had been collecting these things for years and thought a quote of the week would be fun. Most students rushed by the quote on the way to their next class, but gradually people came to expect the new index card each Monday, and several times I was reprimanded politely by students that I was behind in my obligations. I even had an undergraduate, whom I did not know, who would stop, read the quote, and look into the office, giving me a thumbs up when he liked what he had read.

Meanwhile I found myself often teaching courses in translation (epic, tragedy, etc.) and a semester-long honors course for freshmen that was predicated on a Great Books model. Their first semester centered on antiquity, and we read from Homer up through the Roman Empire. Of course, a great deal of time was spent stressing that many of our institutions, art forms, literary genres, and architecture stem from the Greeks and Romans. Yet it was important that students understand that the people of Athens, Sparta, and Rome were not simply older versions of ourselves. In many ways they were extremely strange and distanced from us. Once a year in ancient Rome, live dogs were crucified and paraded about while, in the same parade, geese that had been decorated in purple and gold were carried to the plaudits of the observers. And all this because, when the Gauls invaded Rome circa 390 BCE, the dogs had failed to raise an alarm, but the sacred geese on the Capitoline Hill raised a ruckus. Or consider the fact that once a year, at a religious fertility festival called the Cerealia, Romans tied lighted torches to the tails of foxes and turned them loose in the Circus Maximus for all to see. And the same rational Greeks who solemnly listened to Plato and Aristotle made decisions based on how priests interpreted the flight of birds. They also carved winged, erect phalluses on their door jambs for good luck.

The same Athenians who listened to Socrates in the Agora attended comedies in the theater ten minutes away, where the chorus performed with phalluses dangling from their waist. The philosopher/natural scientist Thales was the first, it is said, to predict a solar eclipse (usually dated to May 28, 585 BCE). But one of the worst defeats ever suffered by an Athenian army occurred on Sicily because a general thought a lunar eclipse was a bad omen. Thus, I often found myself proclaiming to students, "They are not just early versions of ourselves."

The key is in the word "just," for, as my weekly quotes repeatedly showed me, the ancients had the same concerns that all people seem to have had throughout the ages. The Roman comic writer Terence summed it up when he had a character say, "Homo sum; humani nihil a me alienum puto" (I'm a human, and I think that nothing human is alien to me; *Heaut.* 77). A philosopher, slave, king, or subject all have similar concerns no matter where or when they live. What is the right thing to do? How can I be happy? How much wealth is enough? What constitutes success? The answers to such questions appear in many guises. Long answers appear in plays, philosophical works, and modern novels. Shorter answers appear as popular, traditional sayings that, ironically, are often contradictory. Is it "Better safe than sorry," or should one believe, "Nothing ventured, nothing gained"? If "You're never too old to learn," then why is it, "You can't teach an old dog new tricks"?

They Said It First is a way to make clear that ancient Greeks and Romans shared many of the same day to day concerns that we have today. As readers will see, they also shared several of our values, both good and bad. This book is in no way an attempt to present a complete set of quotations or sayings on any given subject. Other books in the past, sadly overlooked today, attempted to do just this. A few of them are listed at the end of this introduction for the curious. Note that many are available online as their copyright long ago ran out. Most of them confine themselves to merely identifying the author of the quote, while some give the work, but usually without a location within the work. Thomas Harbottle's *Dictionary of Quotations (Classical)* is a notable exception and is all the more valuable for that fact.

It is the author's hope that *They Said It First* contains equal amounts of entertainment and enlightenment for all readers, ranging from those with no training in the classics to those, like myself, who have been overly trained. One aim of the current book is to allow the curious to go directly and accurately to the original source. To facilitate this goal, whenever possible, citations and numbering of texts of ancient authors included in this volume are based on the bilingual editions published in the Loeb Classical Library. Fragment numbers not followed by a source represent the numbering used in the Loeb volumes.

A Word of Caution

Finally, a collection of quotations such as this offers a candid look at the values of a society. The same Athenians who valued the beauty of the Parthenon and boasted that they were the "school of Hellas" went home at night to houses run by slaves and wives who were the subject of widely believed biases and very limited freedom. The very inventors of democracy withheld the vote from both these groups as well as from immigrants. The reader is invited to think about such social values in her or his own country and time and, perhaps, come to a more balanced and valid appreciation of where the ancients shone and where they still had work to do—as do we all.

The role a culture's sayings play in helping us understand that culture is important, and Wolfgang Mieder's *Behold the Proverbs of a People: Proverbial Wisdom in Culture, Literature, and Politics* offers a useful and readable overview of the subject.

Quote Books

They Said It First stands at the end of a long line of books collecting quotes of the ancient Greeks and Romans. In fact, many such books existed in antiquity. Ancient grammarians constantly used examples from works and authors that have not survived down to our times. Polymaths like Athenaeus and Aulus Gellius wrote long rambling books, which collected thousands of such quotes. Diogenes Laertius wrote biographies of the philosophers, and these are riddled with pithy sayings purported to be from the mouths of the philosophers. The tendency continued unabated, and Stobaeus, in the fifth century CE, produced a mammoth two volume compendium of extracts from Greek authors that still exists.

A note on quotes from medieval sources: we have left to us a seemingly innumerable number of Latin quotes from an abundance of medieval texts, collected into large volumes such as those of Jakob Werner or Hans Walther. Many sound quite modern: "Plus valet in manibus avis unica fronde duabus" (A single sparrow in your hands is worth more than two on the branch) or "Sumpto gratis equo non os spectare memento" (Remember not to look in the mouth of a horse you have received for free). As intriguing as these are, they do not usually give an ancient predecessor or source. The *Adages* (*Adagia*, also called the *Chiliades*) of Erasmus, however, are to be trusted a bit more as he often does cite sources. Several versions of his work are available online.

Tracking down and authenticating quotes is an iffy proposition, especially in this age of the internet, where a quote falsely attributed to someone once appears hundreds of times and turns into an accepted fact. I have striven, wherever possible, to authenticate all modern quotes. Sometimes this is difficult. Many quotations are falsely attributed to what some have called "quotation magnets," people like Mark Twain, who are known for pithy and memorable sayings. Yogi Berra, one of the best quotation magnets of all time, even entitled one of his books *The Yogi Book: I Really Didn't Say Everything I Said!*

An example seems in order. One of my favorite quotes is "Academic politics are so vicious precisely because the stakes are so small." An internet search of the entire phrase yields a plethora of results, with the quote most often attributed to Henry Kissinger. Such an attribution suits his mordent wit as well as his time in academia. Alas, not only is the wording of the quote variable (at least ten versions exist), but the words have been variously attributed to Henry Kissinger, Wallace Sayre, Charles Frankel, Samuel Johnson, Jesse Unruh, Courtney Brown, and Laurence J. Peter. Likewise, an internet search for "Old age is a shipwreck" and "de Gaulle" yields scores of hits. Searching the same quote on Google Scholar yields attributions to Charles de Gaulle and François-René de Chateaubriand. In the midst of uncertainty, in cases where I could not verify the source of a quote, I have marked it as attributed. Every ancient quote has been checked whenever possible. Modern parallels are taken only from reputable sources that themselves give the source of the quote.

Notes on Using This Book

1. A pronunciation guide for the Greek is offered for those who have not studied the language. See Appendix A: Pronunciation of Greek.

2. A translation is given for every Latin or Greek quote. When called for, the original may be slightly changed. This occurs when the quote is in a subordinate clause and the verb is thus in the subjunctive or infinitive mood. The indicative mood is occasionally substituted for clarity.

3. Citations to ancient authors follow these conventions:

    a. If an author is known for only one work, only the author's name is given.

    b. If the name of the work is given, it is generally abbreviated in accordance with the most common abbreviations used in the *Oxford Classical Dictionary* and the major Greek and Latin lexicons. Works cited, as well as abbreviations used, are listed under the relevant author in Appendix B: Ancient Authors and People Cited. This appendix also supplies biographical information on each ancient author or speaker cited in the book.

4. Line and section numbers generally follow those used in the Loeb Classical Library, published by Harvard University Press. Loeb editions have the ancient language to the left and a facing translation to the right. Many older, out of copyright Loeb editions are available online. Be aware that numbering lines within a work often varies from one edition to the next.

5. Quotes are arranged by topic. Consult the index if you are seeking quotes by a particular author.

6. Many of the quotes, both ancient and modern, are in verse. Due to the need for economy of space, they are given here as continuous prose with conventional capitalization rules applied. A slash (/) is used to indicate the end of a line of poetry. Likewise, words added to the text to help understand it out of context are placed between square brackets. Example: [He used to say that] haste makes waste.

For Further Reading

An asterisk (*) means that the book was available online as of December 2018.

Guterman, Norbert. *A Book of Latin Quotations.* Garden City, NY: Anchor Books, 1966.

*Harbottle, Thomas Benfield. *Dictionary of Quotations (Classical)*. New York: Macmillan, 1897.

Mieder, Wolfgang. *Behold the Proverbs of a People: Proverbial Wisdom in Culture, Literature, and Politics*. Jackson: University Press of Mississippi, 2014.

*Ramage, Craufurd Tait. *Beautiful Thoughts from Latin Authors*. Liverpool: Edward Howell, 1864.

*Riley, Henry T. *Dictionary of Latin and Greek Quotations, Proverbs, Maxims, and Mottos, Classical and Mediaeval, Including Law Terms and Phrases*. London: George Bell and Sons, 1891.

Yeroulanos, Marinos, ed. *A Dictionary of Classical Greek Quotations*. London: I. B. Tauris, 2016.

Abbreviations

An asterisk (*) = cf. Bibliography

b.	born
c.	century
ca.	*circa*, "about"
CAF	Kock*
cf.	*confer*, "compare"
ch.	chapter
d.	died
ed.	editor
D-K	Diels and Kranz*
FCG	Meineke (1839–57)*
fl.	*floruit*, "was at his or her height"
frag.	fragment
K-A	Kassel and Austin*
no.	number
PLG	Bergk*
TGrF	Snell*
vol.	volume

Acceptance

🏛 μὴ ζήτει τὰ γινόμενα γίνεσθαι ὡς
θέλεις, ἀλλὰ θέλε τὰ γινόμενα ὡς
γίνεται καὶ εὑροήσεις.

Do not seek to have events happen as you want them to,
rather wish them to happen as they do happen, and you
will do well.

–Epictetus, *Ench.* 8.

You've got to roll with the punches (*or* go with
the flow).

–Popular saying.

🏛 παλαιὰ καινοῖς δακρύοις οὐ χρὴ
στένειν.

There's no need to groan over things of the past with new tears.

–Euripides, *Alexander* frag. 46 (Collard &
Cropp).

Let bygones be bygones.

–Popular saying.

Don't cry over spilt milk.

–Popular saying.

Adaptability

🏛 Quando hic sum, non ieiuno Sabbato: quando Romae sum, ieiuno Sabbato.

When I am here [in Milan] I do not fast on the Sabbath. When I am at Rome, I do.

–St. Ambrose, quoted in St. Augustine,
Ep. 36.14.

When in Rome do as the Romans do.

–Popular saying.

My heart's in a pickle, it's constantly fickle, and not too partickle, I fear. When I'm not near the girl I love, I love the girl I'm near.

–E.Y. Harburg, "When I'm Not Near the Girl I Love," song in *Finian's Rainbow* (1947).

🏛 Malum est consilium quod mutari non potest.

It is a bad plan that cannot be changed.

–Publilius Syrus 403.

Adapt or die.

–Popular saying.

Anxiety

 οὐδεὶς ἐπὶ σμικροῖσι λυπεῖται σοφός.

No one who is wise gets upset over small things.

–Chaeremon, frag. 37 (*TGrF*).

Don't sweat the small stuff.

–Popular saying.

 Quanta laboras in Charybdi!

How much you labor in Charybdis!

–Horace, *Carm.* 1.27.19. Said to a young
man in the throes of love. Charybdis
was a whirlpool between the "toe"
of Italy and Sicily, made famous in
Homer's *Odyssey*.

You are up to your neck in it.

–Popular saying.

Argument

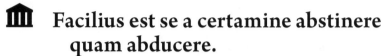 **Facilius est se a certamine abstinere quam abducere.**

It is easier to avoid a quarrel than to get out of one.
—Seneca, *Ira* 3.8.8.

I dislike arguments of any kind. They are always vulgar and often convincing.
—Oscar Wilde, *The Importance of Being Earnest*, act 3 (1895).

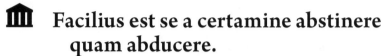 **Nimium altercando veritas amittitur.**

When the arguing is excessive, the truth is lost.
—Publilius Syrus 461.

Perspicuitas enim argumentatione elevatur.

Clear thinking is diminished by debate.
—Cicero, *N.D.* 3.9.

Positive, adj. Mistaken at the top of one's voice.
—Ambrose Bierce, *The Devil's Dictionary* (1911).

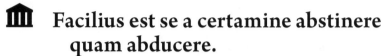 **Cadit statim simultas, ab altera parte deserta: nisi pariter, non pugnant.**

A disagreement fails immediately when it is abandoned by one of the two. Unless it is mutual, they are not fighting.
—Seneca, *Ira* 2.34.5.

Remember, it takes two to make an argument. The one who is wrong is the one who will be doing most of the talking.

–Ann Landers, attributed.

Beauty & the Beast

🏛 **Stultissimus est qui hominem aut ex veste aut ex conditione, quae vestis modo nobis circumdata est, aestimat.**

It is a very stupid man who judges a person either by the clothes he wears or his rank, which is, after all, only a garment wrapped around us.

> –Seneca, *EM* 47.16.

Clothes make the man.

> –Popular saying; cf. "Vestis virum facit" in Erasmus, *Adages* 5.2060.

You can't judge a book by its cover.

> –Popular saying.

🏛 **Taedit te quaedam mala fabula, qua tibi fertur / valle sub alarum trux habitare caper.**

What's hurting your chances is the evil tale that a fierce goat lives in the valley of your armpits.

> –Catullus 69.5–6. Catullus is taunting a rival who is a failure with the ladies, not too subtly suggesting that he has body odor.

To have the goat

> –Popular saying, referring to body odor. Goats can smell quite strong.

Non bene olet, qui bene semper olet.

He who always smells good, doesn't smell good.

–Martial, *Epig.* 2.12.4.

I cannot talk with civet in the room, / a fine puss gentleman that's all perfume.

–William Cowper, "Conversation" (1782).

Calvo turpius est nihil comato.

There is nothing uglier than a bald man with hair.

–Martial, *Epig.* 10.83.11. A fellow named Marinus has a terrible comb-over. Martial says it is ridiculous, especially when the wind blows.

Nobody is really happy with what's on their head. People with straight hair want curly, people with curly want straight, and bald people want everyone to be blind.

–Rita Rudner, "Should I Get My Head Analyzed or Just My Hair?," *Naked Beneath My Clothes* (2001).

Nimis est miseria nimis pulchrum esse hominem.

It is an exceptional curse to be an exceptionally handsome man.

–Plautus, *Mil.* 68. The speaker is the Braggart Soldier, an impossibly vain man.

The curse of beauty
> –Popular saying and the title of James
> Bone's 2016 book about Audrey
> Munson (1891–1996), America's first
> supermodel.

Pride that dines on Vanity sups on Contempt.
> –Benjamin Franklin, *Poor Richard's
> Almanack* (1758).

🏛 κύων κυνὶ / κάλλιστον εἶμεν φαίνεται
καὶ βοῦς βοΐ, / ὄνος δ᾽ ὄνῳ κάλλιστον,
ὗς δέ θην ὑί.

*To a dog, a dog appears most fair; to an ox, an ox; to an ass, an
ass; to a pig, a pig.*
> –Epicharmus, quoted in Diogenes
> Laertius 3.1.16.

Beauty is in the eye of the beholder.
> –Popular saying.

Beginnings

🏛 **Omnium enim rerum principia parva sunt.**

The beginnings of all things are small.

−Cicero, *Fin.* 5.58.

Flumina pauca vides magnis de fontibus orta.

You see few rivers sprung from mighty springs.

−Ovid, *Rem.* 97.

Quidquid futurum est summum ab imo nascitur.

Whatever is going to be the highest arises from the lowest.

−Publilius Syrus 600.

Parva saepe scintilla contempta magnum excitavit incendium.

Often, a tiny spark, overlooked, has given rise to a great fire.

−Quintus Curtius 6.3.11.

Large streams from little fountains flow, tall oaks from little acorns grow.

−English proverb, with many subsequent literary variations.

🏛 **οὐκοῦν οἶσθ᾽ ὅτι ἀρχὴ παντὸς ἔργου μέγιστον;**

Well then, don't you know that the the beginning of every act is the biggest part?

−Plato, *Resp.* 377a.

ἔργου δὲ παντὸς ἤν τις ἄρχηται καλῶς
/ καὶ τὰς τελευτὰς εἰκός ἐσθ᾽ οὕτως
ἔχειν.

*If a person should begin anything well, then it is likely that
the outcome will be the same.*

–Sophocles, frag. 831.

κακῆς ἀπ᾽ ἀρχῆς γίγνεται τέλος κακόν.

From a bad beginning comes a bad end.

–Euripides, *Aeolus* frag. 32.

Foedum inceptu, foedum exitu.

Foul in the beginning, foul at the end.

–Livy 1.10.

GIGO (Garbage in, garbage out)

–Maxim of computer programmers.

Books & Reading

🏛 **Multum legendum esse, non multa.**

One should read greatly, not just many things.

–Pliny the Younger, *Ep.* 7.9.

However, many books, / wise men have said, are
wearisome; who reads / incessantly, and to
his reading brings not a spirit and judgement
equal or superior . . . / uncertain and
unsettled still remains, / deep vers'd in books,
and shallow in himself, / crude or intoxicate,
collecting toys / and trifles for choice matters,
worth a sponge; / as children gathering
pebbles on the shore.

–John Milton, *Paradise Regained*
4.321–30.

🏛 **Optimis adsuescendum est et multa
magis quam multorum lectione
formanda mens.**

*The mind must be formed by reading the best, and not a great
number of authors.*

–Quintilian 10.1.59.

**Non refert quam multos libros, sed
quam bonos habeas; lectio certa
prodest, varia delectat.**

*It doesn't matter how many books you have, but how good
they are. Careful reading is productive, wide reading
delights.*

–Seneca, *EM* 45.1.

The bookful blockhead, ignorantly read, / with loads of learned lumber in his head.

> –Alexander Pope, "An Essay on Criticism" (1711).

Too much reading only produces a pretentious ignoramus.

> –Jean-Jacques Rousseau, *Emile, or On Education*, book 5 (1762).

A man ought to read just as inclination leads him, for what he reads as a task will do him little good.

> –Samuel Johnson, quoted in James Boswell, *Life of Samuel Johnson*, entry for July 14, 1763 (1791).

🏛 μέγα βιβλίον ἴσον ... τῷ μεγάλῳ κακῷ.

A big book is the same as a big bad.

> –Callimachus, quoted in Athenaeus 3.72. Usually given tersely as "A big book is a big evil" or "Big book, big bad."

Another damned thick book! Always scribble, scribble, scribble! Eh, Mr. Gibbon?

> –Attributed to Prince William Henry, Duke of Gloucester and Edinburgh (1781) upon receiving a volume of *The History of the Decline and Fall of the Roman Empire* as a present from Edward Gibbon.

τοὺς θησαυροὺς τῶν πάλαι σοφῶν
ἀνδρῶν, οὓς ἐκεῖνοι κατέλιπον ἐν
βιβλίοις γράψαντες, ἀνελίττων
κοινῇ σὺν τοῖς φίλοις διέρχομαι.

*I unroll the treasures of the wise men of old, which they have left
us in their writings and make my way through them with
my friends.*

–Socrates, quoted in Xenophon, *Mem.*
1.6.14.

The reading of all good books is like
conversation with the finest men of past
centuries.

–René Descartes, *Discourse on Method*
(1639).

Somewhere there are children—Amish
children, classics professors' children,
children in communes—who watch no TV;
all good wishes to them.

–James Kaplan, "Go, Go Power Rangers,"
TV Guide (July 9, 2015).

 Quid est enim dulcius otio literato?

What is sweeter than a scholarly leisure?

–Cicero, *Tusc.* 5.105.

Me, poor man, my library / was dukedom large
enough.

–William Shakespeare, *Tempest,* act 1
scene 2 (1610–11).

🏛 Otium sine litteris mors est et
hominis vivi sepultura.

Leisure without study is the death and burial of a living person.
−Seneca, *EM* 82.4.

Peream, si est tam necessarium quam videtur silentium in studia seposito.

May I die on the spot if anything other than silence seems more necessary for a person who has secluded himself to study.
−Seneca, *EM* 56.1.

For if heuene be on this erthe and ese to any soule / it is in cloistre or in scole by many skilles I fynde / for in cloistre cometh [no] man to chide ne to fighte / but alle is buxomnesse there and bokes to rede and to lerne.
−William Langland, *Piers Plowman*, passus 10 (ca. 1370−90).

🏛 (Dicere enim solebat) nullum esse librum tam malum, ut non aliqua parte prodesset.

He used to say that there is no book so bad that it didn't contain something of use in it.
−Pliny the Elder, quoted in Pliny the Younger, *Ep.* 3.5.10.

"There is no book so bad," said the bachelor, "but something good may be found in it."
−Miguel de Cervantes, *Don Quixote*, part 2, ch. 3 (1605−15).

🏛 **Mihi vero omne tempus est ad meos libros vacuum; numquam enim sunt illi occupati.**

But I always have spare time for my books; for they are never too busy for me.

–Cicero, *Rep.* 1.14.

Books are the quietest and most constant of friends; they are the most accessible and wisest of counsellors, and the most patient of teachers.

–Charles William Eliot, "The Happy Life," an address delivered at The Woman's College, Baltimore (November 7, 1895).

Bragging

🏛 οὐκ ἔστιν οὐδὲν λεγόμενον μακρῶς,
ὅτε / ὁ λέγων ὑποτάττει τοῖς λόγοις
τὰ πράγματα.

Nothing said is bragging if the speaker backs up his words with actions.

–Antiphanes, frag. 46 (*FCG*) (= Stobaeus
34.4).

It ain't bragging if you can do it.

–Dizzy Dean, attributed.

Business & Leisure
(See also Haste, Work)

 Negotium populo Romano melius quam otium committitur.

Work is better entrusted to the Roman people than leisure is.

–Appius Claudius Caecus, quoted in
Valerius Maximus 7.2.1.

Otio qui nescit uti, / plus negoti habet, quam cum est negotium in negotio.

A person who does not know how to use leisure has more business than when working at his business.

–Ennius, *Iphigenia* frag. 84 (= Aulus
Gellius 19.10.12).

To be able to fill leisure intelligently is the last product of civilization.

–Bertrand Russell, *The Conquest of
Happiness*, ch. 14 (1930).

 ἀεργοῖς αἰὲν ἑορτά.

To those who don't work, every day is a holiday.

–Theocritus, *Id.* 15.26.

Easy Street, I'd love to live on Easy Street; nobody works on Easy Street, just lie 'round all day.

–Alan Rankin Jones, "Easy Street," song
(1941).

Multa agendo, nihil agens

Doing a lot, accomplishing nothing
–Phaedrus 2.5.3.

The hurrier I go, the behinder I get.
> –Attributed falsely and widely to the White Rabbit in *Alice's Adventures in Wonderland*, perhaps a corruption of the Red Queen's statement: "'Now, here, you see, it takes all the running you can do, to keep in the same place. If you want to get somewhere else, you must run at least twice as fast as that!'" Lewis Carroll, *Through the Looking Glass*, ch. 2 (1871).

Never mistake activity for achievement.
> –John Wooden, attributed.

Caution

 μία γὰρ χελιδὼν ἔαρ οὐ ποιεῖ.
One swallow doesn't make a spring.
> –Aristotle, *Eth. Nic.* 1098a.

One swallow does not a summer make.
> –Popular saying.

 In plerisque rebus mediocritas optima est.
In most things moderation is best.
> –Cicero, *Off.* 1.130.

Why then, can one desire / too much of a good thing?
> –William Shakespeare, *As You Like It*, act 4 scene 1 (1599–1600).

Too much of a good thing is wonderful.
> –Mae West, quoted by Liberace (seen in a clip from the television show *Reputations*, May 23, 2000).

 Frons occipitio prior est.
The forehead is better than the back of the head.
> –Cato the Elder, *Agr.* 4.1. In other words, it is better to have foresight than hindsight.

Forewarned is forearmed.
> –Popular saying.

🏛 ἥσυχος, ὥσπερ ἐγώ, μέσσην ὁδὸν
ἔρχεο ποσσίν.

Keep your feet quietly in the middle of the road as I do.
—Theognis 331.

Medio tutissimus ibis.

You will go most safely in the middle.
—Ovid, *Met.* 2.137.

*There's Nothing in the Middle of the Road but
Yellow Stripes and Dead Armadillos: A Work of
Political Subversion*
—Jim Hightower, title of book (1998).

Middle-of-the-road
—Popular saying.

🏛 ## Mora omnis odio est sed facit
sapientiam.

All delay is annoying, but it produces wisdom.
—Publilius Syrus 352.

Delay is preferable to error.
—Thomas Jefferson, letter to George
Washington (May 16, 1792).

🏛 ## Cave quicquam incipias quod
paeniteat postea.

Be careful of starting something that you might regret later.
—Publilius Syrus 125.

Mora cogitationis diligentia est.

Delay is diligence of thought.

–Publilius Syrus 390.

Stultus est qui fructus earum spectat, altitudinem non metitur.

He's a fool who looks at [trees'] fruits but doesn't consider their height.

–Quintus Curtius 7.8.14.

Look before you leap.

–Popular saying.

Don't start something you can't finish.

–Popular saying.

καιρῷ λατρεύειν μήδ' ἀντιπνέειν ἀνέμοισιν.

[One must] serve the right moment and not blow against the winds.

–Pseudo-Phocylides, *Sententiae* (*PLG* 2.98). Some change the text to read ἀντιπλέειν, "to sail against."

You don't tug on Superman's cape. You don't spit into the wind. You don't pull the mask off that old Lone Ranger, and you don't mess around with Jim.

–Jim Croce, "You Don't Mess around with Jim," song (1972).

You don't need a weatherman to know which way the wind blows.

–Bob Dylan, "Subterranean Homesick Blues," song (1965).

Noli rogare, quod inpetrare nolueris.

Don't ask for something that you don't want to get.

—Seneca, *EM* 95.1, calling it a *verbum publicum*, a common saying.

Be careful what you wish for.

—Popular saying.

 ## Quod dubites, ne feceris.

When in doubt, don't do it.

—Pliny the Younger, *Ep.* 1.18.5.

Non semper temeritas est felix.

Being bold does not always have a happy ending.

—Livy 28.42.7.

Fools rush in where angels fear to tread.

—Popular saying.

 ## Certa mittimus dum incerta petimus.

We lose what is certain when we seek that which is uncertain.

—Plautus, *Pseud.* 685.

τὰν παρεοῖσαν ἄμελγε· τί τὸν φεύγοντα διώκεις;

Milk the cow near at hand. Why chase someone that is running away?

—Theocritus, *Id.* 11.75.

A bird in the hand is worth two in the bush.

—Popular saying.

🏛 ἀρχόμενον τὸ κακὸν κόπτειν, ἕλκος
τ᾽ ἀκέσασθαι.

Cut out the evil as soon as it has begun and heal the wound.
> –Pseudo-Phocylides, *Sententiae* (*PLG*
> 101).

A stitch in time saves nine.
> –Popular saying.

An ounce of prevention is worth a pound of
cure.
> –Popular saying.

🏛 **Deliberandum est saepe; statuendum
est semel.**

One must deliberate often, decide once.
> –Publilius Syrus 155.

Measure twice, cut once.
> –Popular saying among artisans.

Look before you leap.
> –Popular saying.

🏛 μὴ κίνη χεράδας.

Don't kick the gravel around.
> –Sappho, frag. 145, based on frag. 344
> of Alcaeus, which says that if a man
> disturbs gravel that is unstable, he will
> probably get a headache.

Let sleeping dogs lie.
> –Popular saying.

Serum est cavendi tempus in mediis malis.

Too late being cautious when you are in the middle of difficulties.

–Seneca, *Thy.* 487.

When you're up to your neck in alligators, it's hard to remember that your initial objective was to drain the swamp.

–Popular saying.

Closing the barn door after the horse has bolted

–Popular saying.

Change

🏛 λέγει που Ἡράκλειτος ὅτι πάντα χωρεῖ καὶ οὐδὲν μένει, δὶς ἐς τὸν αὐτὸν ποταμὸν οὐκ ἂν ἐμβαίης.

Heraclitus says, you know, that everything moves and nothing stays static and that you can't step into the same river twice.

–Socrates, quoted in Plato, *Cra.* 401d. The first part is often cited simply as πάντα ῥεῖ.

Panta Rhei

–The name of a Hungarian rock band, various recordings, and the name given to a secret society in Umberto Eco's *Foucault's Pendulum* (1989). Heraclitus's original statement can be seen reflected in the Disney film *Pocahontas* (1995) in the song "Colors of the Wind": "What I love most about rivers is you can't step in the same river twice; the water's always changing, always flowing."

Charity (See also Gratitude)

🏛 **Inopi beneficium bis dat qui dat
celeriter.**

He gives twice who quickly gives to one who is needy.

> –Publilius Syrus 274. Usually just cited
> as "Bis dat qui cito dat"; cf. Erasmus,
> *Adages* 1.8.91.

**Si bene quid facias, facias cito; nam cito
factum, gratum erit; ingratum gratia
tarda facit.**

*If you are going to do anything good, do it quickly; for a
good deed done quickly will be received with gratitude.
Slow benevolence only creates ingratitude.*

> –Ausonius, *Epig.* 17.

My friends, Dr. King realized that the only real
wealth comes from helping others.

> –César Chávez, "Lessons of Dr. Martin
> Luther King, Jr.," speech (1990).

🏛 **Improbus est homo qui beneficium
scit sumere, et reddere nescit.**

*It's a foul fellow who knows how to accept a good deed but not
how to return one.*

> –Plautus, *Per.* 762.

Feeling gratitude and not expressing it is like
wrapping a present and not giving it.

> –William Arthur Ward, widely attributed,
> famous author of maxims.

🏛 ## Qui beneficium dedit, taceat, narret qui accepit.

When one has done a good deed, let him keep quiet about it.
Let the one who received it speak of it.

–Seneca, *Ben.* 2.11.2.

Qui beneficium dedit, oblivisci oportet.

One who has bestowed a favor should forget about it.

–Seneca, *Ben.* 7.22.1.

The best philanthropy is anonymous charity. . . .
The higher giving is anonymous giving.

–Gene Simmons (of rock band Kiss),
interview with Radio.com (July 6,
2016).

Don't blow your own horn.

–Popular saying.

🏛 ## Quod tuum est meum est; omne meum est autem tuum.

What's yours is mine. Everything that's mine is yours.

–Plautus, *Trin.* 229.

ἐν γὰρ ξυνῷ ἰχθύι ἄκανθαι οὐκ ἔνεισιν.

There are no bones in a shared fish.

–Democritus, frag. 151 (D-K).

Mi casa es su casa. (My house is your house.)

–Popular saying, taken from a Spanish
proverb.

Consequences

 Qui in unguentaria taberna resederunt et paullo diutius commorati sunt, odorem secum loci ferunt.

Those who have spent time in a perfumer's shop and have stayed there a while take away with themselves the smell of the place.

−Seneca, *EM* 108.4.

Qui in solem venit . . . colorabitur.

One who walks into the sunlight will get sunburned.

−Seneca, *EM* 108.4.

Lie down with dogs, get up with fleas

−Popular saying.

Consistency

🏛 **Nemo doctus umquam . . .**
mutationem consili inconstantiam
dixit esse.

No one with brains ever said that a change of mind is a sign of
inconsistency.

–Cicero, *Att.* 415.2.

This imputation of inconsistency is one to which
every sound politician and every honest
thinker must sooner or later subject himself.
The foolish and the dead alone never change
their opinion.

–James Russell Lowell, "Abraham
Lincoln," *My Study Windows*
(1899).

🏛 **Gravissimum est imperium**
consuetudinis.

The rule of habit is a very great burden.

–Publilius Syrus 236.

A foolish consistency is the hobgoblin of
little minds, adored by little statesmen and
philosophers and divines. With consistency
a great soul has simply nothing to do.

–Ralph Waldo Emerson, *Self Reliance*
(1841).

Cooperation

🏛 οὐδὲ γὰρ ἄνευ σμικρῶν τοὺς μεγάλους
φασὶν οἱ λιθολόγοι λίθους εὖ
κεῖσθαι.

*As the masons say, the large stones don't sit well in place
without the small ones.*

–Plato, *Leg.* 902e.

You just call on me, brother, when you need a
hand; we all need somebody to lean on.

–Bill Withers, "Lean on Me," song (1972).

🏛 ἁ δὲ χεὶρ τὰν χεῖρα νίζει· δός τι, καὶ
λάβοις τι.

*Hand washes hand; give something and you might get
something.*

–Epicharmus, frag. 30 (D-K).

χεὶρ χεῖρα νίπτει, δάκτυλοι δὲ δακτύλους.

Hand washes hand, finger fingers.

–Menander, frag. 832 (Jäkel).

Manus manum lavat.

Hand washes hand.

–Seneca, *Apoc.* 9; Petronius 46.

Mutuum muli scalpant.

One mule scratches the other.

–Ausonius, *Technop.* 4.12.

One hand washes the other.
–Popular saying.

You scratch my back, I'll scratch yours.
–Popular saying.

Courage & Fear

🏛 Leo a leporibus insultatur
mortuus.

A lion is taunted by hares—once it's dead.
> −Publilius Syrus, in some collections.

You are the hare of whom the proverb goes, /
whose valor plucks dead lions by the beard.
> −William Shakespeare, *King John*, act 2
> scene 1 (1596).

🏛 θαρσαλέα δὲ παρὰ κρατῆρα φωνὰ
γίνεται.

One's voice grows bold in the wine bowl.
> −Pindar, *Nem.* 9.49.

Dutch courage
> −Popular saying, originating perhaps
> from the Anglo-Dutch Wars when
> soldiers imbibed jenever (gin) before
> battle.

🏛 Audendo magnus tegitur timor.

Great fear is masked by daring.
> −Lucan 4.702.

Fake it till you make it.
> −Popular saying.

🏛 ἀνὴρ ὁ φεύγων καὶ πάλιν μαχήσεται.

A man who runs away will fight again.

> –Menander, *Mon.* 45.

For he who fights and runs away / may live to fight another day; / but he who is in battle slain / can never rise and fight again.

> –Oliver Goldsmith, *The Art of Poetry on a New Plan* 2.147 (1761); cf. John Mennes and James Smith, *Musarum Deliciae* (1656).

🏛 **In rebus asperis et tenui spe fortissima quaeque consilia tutissima sunt.**

When times are tough and hope is in short supply, the boldest plans are the safest ones.

> –Livy 25.38.18.

When the going gets tough, the tough get going.

> –Popular saying.

🏛 **Tanta adeo cum res trepidae reverentia divum, / nascitur.**

It is when matters are troubled that this kind of great reverence for the gods is born.

> –Silius Italicus 7.88–89.

Adversae deinde res admonuerunt religionum.

Adverse circumstances then put us [the Romans] in mind of religion.

> –Livy 5.51.9.

There are no atheists in foxholes.

> –Popular saying, perhaps originating from a sermon given by Chaplain William Thomas Cummings to soldiers before the Battle of Bataan (1942).

🏛 ## Canis timidus vehementius latrat quam mordet: altissima quaeque flumina minimo sono labuntur.

A cowardly dog barks harder than it bites, and the deepest rivers flow with the least sound.

> –Quintus Curtius 7.4.13, quoting a popular Bactrian saying.

His bark is worse than his bite.

> –Popular saying.

Still waters run deep.

> –Popular saying.

🏛 ## A cane non magno saepe tenetur aper.

A boar is often held by a none too big dog.

> –Ovid, *Rem.* 422.

It's not the size of the dog in the fight, it's the size of the fight in the dog.

> –Anonymous, often misattributed to Mark Twain. Quoted by President Dwight D. Eisenhower in a speech before the RNC breakfast (January 31, 1952). Also quoted in the film *Rudy* (1993).

Audentes deus ipse iuvat.
God personally helps the bold.
                    −Ovid, *Met.* 10.586.

Fortis fortuna adiuvat.
Fortune aids the brave.
                    −Terence, *Phorm.* 203.

Audentis fortuna iuvat.
Fortune aids those who dare.
                    −Vergil, *Aen.* 10.284.

Eventus docuit fortes fortunam iuvare.
The event taught us that fortune aids the bold.
                    −Livy 8.29.5.

God helps those who help themselves.
                    −Popular saying.

Audendo virtus crescit, tardando timor.
Courage grows through daring, fear through delaying.
                    −Publilius Syrus 43.

Nemo timendo ad summum pervenit locum.
No one gets to the top by being fearful.
                    −Publilius Syrus 471.

He who hesitates is lost.
                    −Popular saying.

ταράσσει τοὺς ἀνθρώπους οὐ τὰ πράγματα, ἀλλὰ τὰ περὶ τῶν πραγμάτων δόγματα.

Things do not upset people, it's rather their opinions about the things.

−Epictetus, *Ench.* 5.

Maior ignotarum rerum est terror.

Greatest is the terror of unknown things.

−Livy 28.44.3.

Semper plus metuit animus ignotum malum.

The mind always fears most an unknown evil.

−Publilius Syrus 655.

Pericla timidus etiam quae non sunt videt.

A timid soul sees dangers that are not even there.

−Publilius Syrus 500.

Omne ignotum pro magnifico est.

Everything that is unknown is taken as grand.

−Tacitus, *Agr.* 30.3.

Present fears / are less than horrible imaginings.

−William Shakespeare, *Macbeth*, act 1 scene 3 (1606).

Thus, fear of danger is ten thousand times more terrifying than danger itself.

−Daniel Defoe, *Robinson Crusoe*, ch. 11 (1719).

The oldest and strongest emotion of mankind is
fear, and the oldest and strongest kind of fear
is fear of the unknown.

> –H. P. Lovecraft, *Supernatural Horror in
> Literature* (1927).

εἰώθει δὲ λέγειν ὅτι φοβερώτερόν
ἐστιν ἐλάφων στρατόπεδον
ἡγουμένου λέοντος ἢ λεόντων
ἐλάφου.

He [Chabrias] used to say that an army of deer led by a lion is
more frightening than an army of lions led by a deer.

> –Plutarch, *Apoph. bas.* 187d.

In magnis et voluisse sat est.

In great endeavors, just to have had the desire is enough.

> –Propertius 2.10.6

Ut desint vires, tamen est laudanda voluntas.

Though the strength might not be there, the will should still
be praised.

> –Ovid, *Pont.* 3.4.79.

They never fail who die in a great cause.

> –Lord Byron (George Gordon), *Marino
> Faliero*, act 2 scene 2 (1821).

The brave man is not he who does not feel afraid,
but he who conquers that fear.

> –Nelson Mandela, *Long Walk to Freedom*
> (1994).

ἐχθίστη δὲ ὀδύνη ἐστὶ τῶν ἐν
ἀνθρώποισι αὕτη, πολλὰ φρονέοντα
μηδενὸς κρατέειν.

*The most hateful pain that exists for people is to know much
and have power over nothing.*

–Herodotus 9.16.

In depression this faith in deliverance, in
ultimate restoration, is absent. The pain is
unrelenting, and what makes the condition
intolerable is the foreknowledge that no
remedy will come—not in a day, an hour, a
month, or a minute.

–William Styron, *Darkness Visible* (1990).

 **Timidus vocat se cautum, avarus
parcum.**

The coward calls himself cautious; the miser, frugal.

–Publilius Syrus, in some collections.

Matrem timidi flere non solet.

The mother of a timid man seldom has reason to weep.

–Thrasybulus, quoted in Cornelius
Nepos, *Thr.* 8.2.4.

The real hero is the man who fights even though
he is scared.

–General George S. Patton, speech to the
Third Army (June 5, 1944).

Danger

🏛 Numquam periclum sine periclo
vincitur.

Danger is never overcome without danger.
> –Publilius Syrus 428.

He that will not sail till all dangers are over must
never put to sea.
> –Thomas Fuller, *Gnomologia,* no. 2353
> (1732).

🏛 Inter vepres rosae nascuntur et inter
feras nonnullae mitescunt.

*Roses are born amid the brambles and some among the wild
beasts grow tame.*
> –Ammianus Marcellinus 16.7.4.

Spina etiam grata est ex qua spectatur
rosa.

Even a thorn is welcome when the rose is seen.
> –Publilius Syrus 669.

Every rose has its thorn just like every night has
its dawn, just like every cowboy sings his sad,
sad song. Every rose has its thorn.
> –Brett Michaels, C. C. DeVille, Bobby
> Dall, and Rikki Rockett (of rock band
> Poison), "Every Rose Has Its Thorn,"
> song (1988).

Death

 τὸν τεθνηκότα μὴ κακολογεῖν.
Don't speak badly of one who is dead.

> –Chilon, quoted in Diogenes Laertius
> 1.3.70.

Don't speak ill of the dead.

> –Popular saying.

 πολιαὶ στέφουσι κάραν· / δὸς ὕδωρ,
βάλ᾽ οἶνον, ὦ παῖ· / τὴν ψυχήν μου
κάρωσον. / βραχὺ μὴ ζῶντα
καλύπτεις. / ὁ θανὼν οὐκ ἐπιθυμεῖ.
Gray hairs crown my head. Give me water and add wine, boy!
Make my spirit dull! Soon you will bury me, no longer alive;
and the dead man has no desires.

> –*Anacreontea* 52.4 (Loeb, *Greek Lyric II*).

Upon the grave which swallows fast, 'tis peace at
last, oh peace at last.

> –James Hetfield (of band Metallica),
> "Cyanide," song (2007–8).

 **Moriendum enim certe est; et id
incertum an eo ipso die.**
To have to die is certain; what's uncertain is whether it might
happen this very day.

> –Cicero, *Sen.* 74.

Stultum est timere, quod vitari non potest.

It is foolish to fear what can't be avoided.

–Publilius Syrus, in some collections.

The only sure things are death and taxes.

–Popular saying.

🏛 Quod autem omnibus necesse est, idne miserum esse uni potest?

But can that which is necessary for everyone be wretched for a single person?

–Cicero, *Tusc.* 1.119.

Death is a black camel, which kneels at the gates of all.

–Abdelkader, reported in Jehiel Keeler Hoyt, ed., *The Cyclopædia of Practical Quotations* (1882).

🏛 γίγνωσκε δὲ / ὡς πᾶσιν ἡμῖν κατθανεῖν ὀφείλεται.

Know that dying is a debt we all owe.

–Euripides, *Alc.* 418–19.

Reddenda terrae est terra, tum vita omnibus / metenda, ut fruges.

Earth must be returned to earth, and then everyone's life must be reaped like crops.

–Cicero, *Tusc.* 3.60, citing Euripides's lost play *Hypsipyla* as the source.

Omnia mors aequat.

Death makes all things equal.

–Claudian, *Rape of Persephone* 2.302.

Aequat omnes cinis. Inpares nascimur, pares morimur.

Ashes makes everyone equal. Unequal we are born, equal we die.

–Seneca, *EM* 91.16.

Death is the great equalizer.

–Popular saying.

 ### ἀρετὴ δὲ, κἂν θάνῃ τις, οὐκ ἀπόλλυται / … κακοῖσι δὲ / ἅπαντα φροῦδα συνθαόνθ' ὑπὸ / χθονός.

Virtue, even if someone dies, is not destroyed … for base men, though, everything dies along with them beneath the earth.

–Euripides, *Temenidae* frag. 734.

The evil that men do lives after them; / the good is oft interred with their bones.

–William Shakespeare, *Julius Caesar* act 3 scene 2 (1599).

 ### τὸν ἕτερον πόδα ἐν τῷ πορθμείῳ

One foot in the ferry boat

–Lucian, *Apol.* 1, referring to the ferry boat of Charon, who was said to convey souls into the afterlife.

One foot in the grave

–Popular saying.

🏛 **Cineri gloria sera venit.**

Glory comes late for ashes.

–Martial, *Epig.* 1.25.8. Martial is
encouraging a hesitant author to
publish his work and not wait for
posthumous glory.

Those honours come too late / that on our ashes
wait.

–Richard Lovelace, *Posthumous
Poems*, title page (1659). Lovelace is
translating the Martial epigram.

🏛 **Effugit mortem quisquis
contempserit.**

Whoever has scorned death has escaped it.

–Quintus Curtius 4.14.25.

**Crudelius est quam mori semper
mortem timere.**

Constantly fearing death is crueler than dying.

–Seneca the Elder, *Controv.* 3.5.

Cotidie damnatur qui semper timet.

Daily doomed is he who is always afraid.

–Publilius Syrus 112.

Cowards die many times before their deaths; /
the valiant never taste of death but once.

–William Shakespeare, *Julius Caesar*, act
2 scene 2 (1599).

Male vivet quisquis nesciet bene mori.

One who will not know how to die well will not live well.
–Seneca, *Tranq.* 11.4.

Wish not so much to live long as to live well.
–Benjamin Franklin, *Poor Richard's Almanack* (1738).

 ## Prima quae vitam dedit hora, carpit.

The very first hour that bestowed life plucks it away.
–Seneca, *Herc. F.* 874.

Of course you're dying. We're all dying. Where the devil else do you think you're heading?
–Joseph Heller, *Catch-22* (1961).

Dignity

🏛 **Etiam capillus unus habet umbram suam.**

Even a single hair has its own shadow.
> –Publilius Syrus 186.

Every dog has its day.
> –Popular saying.

🏛 **In tauros Libyci fremunt leones; non sunt papilionibus molesti.**

The lions of Libya rage at bulls; they don't bother butterflies.
> –Martial, *Epig.* 12.61.5.

Being powerful is like being a lady. If you have to tell people you are, you aren't.
> –Jesse Carr, head of Teamsters Union Local 959, quoted in *Newsweek* (September 27, 1976).

Diplomacy

 ἐν μεγάλοις πᾶσιν ἀδεῖν χαλεπόν.

Amid weighty affairs, it is hard to please everyone.

–Solon, quoted in Plutarch, *Sol.* 25.6.

βούλου δ' ἀρέσκειν πᾶσι, μὴ σαυτῷ
μονόν.

Wish to be pleasing to all, not just to yourself.

–Menander, *Mon.* 76.

Well, it's all right now, I learned my lesson well.
You see, ya can't please everyone, so ya got to
please yourself.

–Ricky Nelson, "Garden Party," song
(1972).

Eagerness

 δακὼν δὲ στόμιον ὡς νεοζυγὴς / πῶλος
βιάζῃ καὶ πρὸς ἡνίας μάχῃ

Like a fresh-bridled colt who bites at the bit and fights the reins

–Aeschylus, *PV* 1009.

Champing at the bit

–Popular saying.

Education

 ἀναφαίρετον κτῆμ' ἐστὶ παιδεία
βροτοῖς.

*Education is a possession that cannot be taken away from
mortals.*

–Menander, *Mon.* 2.

The beautiful thing about learning is nobody
can take it away from you.

–B. B. King, quoted in the *Charlotte
Observer* (October 5, 1997).

 γηράσκω δ' αἰεὶ πολλὰ διδασκόμενος.

I grow old, ever learning many things.

–Solon, quoted in Plutarch, *Sol.* 31.3.

**Tamdiu discendum est, quamdiu
nescias; si proverbio credimus,
quamdiu vivas.**

*If we are to trust the proverb, then as long as there is
something you do not know you must learn as long as
you live.*

–Seneca, *EM* 76.3.

Ancora imparo. (I'm still learning.)

–Michelangelo, attributed; supposedly
said at age eighty-seven.

Veni igitur, si vir es, et disce a me προλεγομένας quas quaeris; etsi sus Minervam.

Therefore, come along, if you are man enough, and learn the basic principles you seek, even if it is like a pig teaching Minerva.

> –Cicero, *Fam.* 191.3. The shorthand phrase "sus Minervam" was used to show an impossible teaching situation. Cicero, of course, is being falsely modest.

Education is the process of casting fake pearls before real swine.

> –Variously phrased; attributed, probably falsely, to either Irwin Edman or Oliver Wendell Holmes.

Efficiency

 Duo parietes de eadem fidelia dealbare

To whitewash two walls from the same pail
–Cicero, *Fam.* 264.2.

Uno in saltu lepide apros capiam duos.

I'll neatly catch two boars in a single thicket.
–Plautus, *Cas.* 476.

To kill two birds with one stone

–Popular saying.

Excitement

 Excitabat enim fluctus in simpulo,
ut dicitur.

He raised waves in a ladle, as the saying goes.

–Cicero, *Leg.* 3.36.

A tempest in a teapot

–Popular saying.

Experience

 Experientia docet.

Experience is a teacher.

—Based on Tacitus, *Hist.* 5.6.

Experience is the best teacher.

—Popular saying.

 παθὼν δέ τε νήπιος ἔγνω.

The fool knows after he has suffered.

—Hesiod, *Op.* 218.

νηπίοισιν οὐ λόγος, ἀλλὰ ξυμφορὴ γίνεται διδάσκαλος.

For the foolish it is not talk but misfortune that is the teacher.

—Democritus, frag. B32 (D-K).

Stultorum eventus magister est.

The outcome is the teacher of fools.

—Livy 22.39.

Learn the hard way

—Popular saying.

School of hard knocks

—Popular saying.

 ὁ γὰρ μανθάνων κιθαρίζειν κιθαρίζων.

A person learning to play the harp learns by playing the harp.

—Aristotle, *Metaph.* 1049b.

I have but one lamp by which my feet are
guided, and that is the lamp of experience.
—Patrick Henry, speech at the Virginia
Convention (March 23, 1775).

οὐ τόνδ᾿ ἀγῶνα πρῶτον ἂν δράμοίμ᾿ ἐγώ.

This wouldn't be the first race I have run.
—Euripides, *Alc.* 489.

This isn't my first rodeo.
—Popular saying.

Est rerum omnium magister usus.

Experience is the teacher of all.
—Julius Caesar, *B Civ.* 2.8.3.

ἃ γὰρ δεῖ μαθόντας ποιεῖν, ταῦτα ποιοῦντες μανθάνομεν.

What we have to learn to do, we learn by doing.
—Aristotle, *Eth. Nic.* 1103a.

In omnibus fere minus valent praecepta quam experimenta.

In almost all cases rules are less valuable than experience.
—Quintilian 2.5.15.

Experience is the only teacher, and we get his
lesson indifferently in any school.
—Ralph Waldo Emerson, *Journals* (1845).

Family

🏛 **Meos tam suspicione quam crimine iudico carere oportere.**

I think that my family members should be as free from the suspicion of wrongdoing as they are of the accusation of one.

–Suetonius, *Iul.* 74.2.

"ὅτι," ἔφη, "τὴν ἐμὴν ἠξίουν μηδὲ ὑπονοηθῆναι."

"Because," he said, "I thought my wife should not even be under suspicion."

–Plutarch, *Caes.* 10.6. Caesar's second wife Pompeia was suspected of having an affair with a notorious playboy of the time named Clodius. He gave this reason when asked why he divorced her.

Caesar's wife must be above suspicion.

–Popular saying, used to indicate that even a whiff of scandal should be enough to cause public figures to resign from office.

🏛 **Ferme acerrima proximorum odia sunt.**

Just about the fiercest hatred is that of relatives.

–Tacitus, *Hist.* 4.70.

All happy families resemble one another; every unhappy family is unhappy in its own way.

–Leo Tolstoy, *Anna Karenina*, part 1, ch. 1 (1875–77).

Familiarity breeds contempt—and children.
> –Mark Twain, quoted in Albert Paine,
> ed., *Mark Twain's Notebook* (1935).

If a man's character is to be abused, say what you will, there's nobody like a relative to do the business.
> –William Makepeace Thackeray, *Vanity Fair*, ch. 19 (1847–48).

🏛 κασιγνήτῳ γελάσας ἐπὶ μάρτυρα θέσθαι.

[When making a deal,] smile at your brother but get a witness.
> –Hesiod, *Op.* 371.

Entre dos hermanos, dos testigos y un notario (Between two brothers—two witnesses and one notary public)
> –Spanish proverb.

🏛 **Longe fugit quisquis suos fugit.**

He flees far, who flees from his family.
> –Petronius 43.

After a good dinner one can forgive anybody, even one's own relations.
> –Oscar Wilde, *A Woman of No Importance*, act 2 (1893).

🏛 **Heredis fletus sub persona risus est.**

The weeping of an heir is a smile under a mask.
> –Publilius Syrus 1258.

Say not you know another entirely till you have divided an inheritance with him.

> –Johann Kaspar Lavater, *Aphorisms on Man* (ca. 1788).

🏛 προγόνοις δάμαρτες δυσμενεῖς ἀεί ποτε.

Wives are always hostile to children from a previous marriage.

> –Euripides, *Ion* 1329.

Times soon grew very bad for the poor stepchild.

> –Jacob and Wilhelm Grimm, "Aschenputtel/Cinderella," no. 21, *Kinder- und Hausmärchen,* 7th edition, trans. D. L. Ashliman (original work published 1857). The trope of the evil stepmother is found in such ancient stories as those concerning Phaedra and Hippolytus. Hera/Juno herself is often depicted as a wicked stepmother.

🏛 δεινότερον οὐδὲν ἄλλο μητρυῖας κακόν.

Nothing is a more terrifying evil than a mother-in-law.

> –Menander, *Mon.* 127.

Once, long ago, there was one good mother-in-law, but a wolf ate her.

> –French proverb, quoted in Mineke Schipper, *Never Marry a Woman with Big Feet: Women in Proverbs from around the World* (2003).

Fate

🏛 **Passibus ambiguis Fortuna volubilis errat . . . et manet in nullo certa tenaxque loco.**

Fickle fortune wanders with unreliable steps and stays certain and firm in no one place.

–Ovid, *Tr.* 5.8.15.

Ratione mortalium [Fortuna] sola utramque paginam facit.

It is Fortune alone who completes both pages in a mortal's account book.

–Pliny the Elder 2.22.

Fame is a fickle food / upon a shifting plate.

–Emily Dickinson, "Fame is a Fickle Food" (first published 1914).

Sun don't shine on the same dog's ass every day, but, mister you ain't seen a ray of light since you got here.

–Spoken by Fern Persons playing Opal Fleener, *Hoosiers*, film (1986); based on a common expression in the American South. Screenplay by Angelo Pizzo.

σκοπέειν χρὴ παντὸς χρήματος
τὴν τελευτήν, κῇ ἀποβήσεται·
πολλοῖσι γὰρ δὴ ὑποδέξας ὄλβον ὁ
θεὸς προρρίζους ἀνέτρεψε.

*One must look to the end of everything as to how it will turn
out. God has shown happiness to many and then utterly
ruined them.*

–Solon, quoted in Herodotus 1.32. The
wealthy Lydian king Croesus hopes
that Solon will identify him as the
luckiest man on earth. Solon lists
others, however, saying that disaster
can befall anyone up until the day he
dies.

It ain't over until it's over.

–Yogi Berra, *The Yogi Book* (1998).

It ain't over till the fat lady sings.

–Popular saying.

 **Nec enim poterat fieri ut ventus bonis
viris secundus, contrarius malis.**

*It wasn't possible for it to happen that the same wind be
favorable for good people and contrary to the wicked.*

–Seneca, *Ben.* 4.28.3.

It's an ill wind that blows no good.

–Popular saying.

The only thing I ever learned was that some
people are lucky and other people aren't and
not even a graduate of the Harvard Business
School can say why.
> –Kurt Vonnegut, *The Sirens of Titan*
> (1959).

🏛 ἀνερρίφθω κύβος.

Let the die be cast.
> –Julius Caesar, quoted in Plutarch, *Pomp.*
> 50.

Iacta alea est.

The die is cast.
> –Suetonius, *Iul.* 32. Both authors are
> referring to 49 BCE, when Caesar
> crossed the Rubicon River with his
> army under arms, virtually declaring
> war on Pompey. Usually misquoted as
> "Alea iacta est."

"Que Será, Será (Whatever Will Be, Will Be)"
> –Jay Livingston and Ray Evans, title of
> song (1956); made famous by Doris
> Day in Alfred Hitchcock's *The Man
> Who Knew Too Much* (1956). As a
> popular saying, often simply "Que
> será."

🏛 ## Ducunt volentem fata, nolentem trahunt.

The Fates lead a willing person, the unwilling they drag.
> –Seneca, *EM* 107.11.

What fates impose, that men must needs abide;
/ it boots not to resist both wind and tide.

> –William Shakespeare, *Henry VI Part 3*,
> act 4 scene 3 (1591).

 ## Nulli est homini perpetuum bonum.

No one has everlasting good.

> –Plautus, *Curc.* 189.

τῶν ὄντων τὰ μέν ἐστιν ἐφ' ἡμῖν, τὰ δὲ οὐκ ἐφ' ἡμῖν.

Of all there is, some things are up to us and some are not up to us.

> –Epictetus, *Ench.* 1, opening words.

God, grant me the serenity to accept the things I cannot change, courage to change the things I can, and wisdom to know the difference.

> –Reinhold Niebuhr, "Serenity Prayer"
> (1934); adopted in the modified form
> given here by Alcoholics Anonymous
> (1941).

Faults

 Qui culpae ignoscit uni, suadet
pluribus.

*A person who forgives one person's offence encourages many
more.*

–Publilius Syrus 587.

I'm so modest, I can admit my own faults
and my only fault is I don't realize how great
I really am.

–Muhammed Ali; of uncertain date, but
an audio clip is used in an iPhone X
commercial (2018).

 Vitia erunt donec homines.

As long as there are people there will be human failings.

–Tacitus, *Hist.* 4.74.

The best of men are but men at best.

–English proverb.

 Nihil peccat, nisi quod nihil peccat.

He has no faults, except that he has no faults.

–Pliny the Younger, *Ep.* 9.26.1.

Few things are harder to put up with than the
annoyance of a good example.

–Mark Twain, *Pudd'nhead Wilson,*
epigraph to ch. 18 (1894).

Fine Arts

 ὁ βίος βραχὺς, ἡ δὲ τέχνη μακρή.
Life is short, skill/craft is long.

—Hippocrates, *Aphorisms* 1.1.

**Inde illa maximi medicorum
exclamatio est: vitam brevem esse,
longam artem.**
*Thus we have that proclamation of the greatest of physicians
that life is short, art long.*

—Seneca, *Brev. vit.* 1.

Ars longa, vita brevis. (Art is long, life short.)

—This common modern phrase is a
Latin version, and a reversal, of
Hippocrates's statement. It does not
appear in ancient Latin authors. The
actual meaning of Hippocrates's
original is disputed and the Latin
version in circulation today is
generally taken to mean that one's art
outlives the artist.

 ἡ τέχνη μιμεῖται τὴν φυσίν.
Art imitates nature.

—Aristotle, *Ph.* 194a.

I don't want life to imitate art. I want life to
be art.

—Carrie Fisher, *Postcards from the Edge*
(1987).

🏛 ## Omnis ars naturae imitatio est.

All art is the imitation of nature.

–Seneca, *EM* 65.3.

In the vaunted works of Art / the master stroke
is Nature's part.

–Ralph Waldo Emerson, "Nature II,"
May-Day and Other Pieces (1867).

🏛 ## Poeticam istud licentiam decet.

That sort of thing is only fitting for poetic licence.

–Seneca, *Q Nat.* 2.44.1. Criticizing Ovid,
Met. 3.305–7, where the poet claims
that Jupiter had a different, gentler
lightning bolt at his disposal.

And if the tale just told seems a little tall,
remember a thing called poetic license—and
another thing called the Twilight Zone.

–*The Twilight Zone*, "The Bard," season
4 episode 18 (aired May 23, 1963).
Written by Rod Serling.

🏛 ## Non omnes qui habent citharam sunt citharoedi.

Everyone with a lyre isn't a lyre player.

–Varro, *Rust.* 2.1.3.

All that glisters is not gold.

–William Shakespeare, *Merchant of
Venice*, act 2 scene 7 (1596–97).

🏛 # Citharoedus ridetur chorda qui semper oberrat eadem.

A lyre player who always makes a mistake on the same string is laughed at.

–Horace, *Ars P.* 355–56.

Don't make the same mistake twice!

–Popular saying.

🏛 # Non datur ad Musas currere lata via.

To run to the Muses on a wide highway is not just given as a gift.

–Propertius 3.1.14.

If I don't practice one day, I know it; two days, the critics know it; three days, the public knows it.

–Attributed to Jascha Heifetz, violinist, or Ignacy Jan Paderewski, pianist.

🏛 # Omnium magnarum artium, sicut arborum, altitudo nos delectat, radices stirpesque non item; sed esse illa sine his non potest.

The loftiness of all great arts, like that of trees, delights us, but not their roots and stems. Yet, without the latter, the former could not exist.

–Cicero, *Orat.* 147.

Excuse me, how do you get to Carnegie Hall?
Practice, my boy. Practice.

–Old joke.

🏛 Omnia non pariter rerum sunt omnibus apta.

All things are not suitable for all people.

> –Propertius 3.9.7. Propertius is responding to Maecenas, Augustus's minister of the arts. Maecenas had asked Propertius to write an epic glorifying Rome. Propertius demurs, adding "non sunt apta meae grandia vela rati" (great sails are not suitable for my little boat).

Knowing what you cannot do is more important than knowing what you can do.

> –Lucille Ball, quoted in Eleanor Harris, *The Real Story of Lucille Ball* (1954).

🏛 Nullum magnum ingenium sine mixtura dementiae fuit.

No great genius has ever existed without a touch of madness.

> –Seneca, *Tranq.* 17.10. Aristotle dealt with the issue (*Problems* 30.1) although this is not a translation from his Greek.

There's a fine line between genius and insanity. I have erased this line.

> –Oscar Levant, quoted in Cleveland Amory, *Celebrity Register: An Irreverent Compendium of American Quotable Notables* (1959).

🏛 μήτι τοι δρυτόμος μέγ᾽ ἀμείνων ἠὲ
βίηφι.

*The woodcutter, you know, is far better for his skill than he is for
his strength.*

–Homer, *Il.* 23.315.

'Tis God gives skill, / but not without men's
hands: He could not make / Antonio
Stradivari's violins / without Antonio.

–George Eliot, "Stradivarius" (1873).

Food & Drink

Food

🏛 οὐ μὲν γάρ τι χέρειον ἐν ὥρῃ δεῖπνον
ἑλέσθαι.

Nothing is any the worse when meals are taken on time.

–Homer, *Od.* 17.176.

Strange to see how a good dinner and feasting
reconciles everybody.

–Samuel Pepys, *Diary*, entry for
November 9, 1665 (1825).

🏛 **Socratem audio dicentem, cibi
condimentum esse famem,
potionis sitim.**

*I hear Socrates saying that hunger is the spice of food and thirst
of drink.*

–Cicero, *Fin.* 2.90.

La mejor salsa del mundo es la hambre. (Hunger
is the best sauce in the world.)

–Miguel de Cervantes, *Don Quixote*, part
3, ch. 5 (1605–15).

Der Hunger is der beste Koch. (Hunger is the
best cook.)

–German saying.

Our stomachs / will make what's homely savory.

–William Shakespeare, *Cymbeline*, act 3
scene 6 (1610).

Ieiunus raro stomachus vulgaria temnit.

An empty stomach rarely looks askance at common food.
–Horace, *Sat.* 2.2.38.

Beggars can't be choosers.
–Popular saying.

Fabas indulcet fames. (Hunger sweetens beans.)
–A proverb in use since at least the nineteenth century but not of classical origin. Today the Latin is widely used for such things as tattoos, tee shirts, and coffee mugs.

 ## Ab ovo usque ad mala

From egg all the way to apples/fruit
–Horace, *Sat.* 1.3.6. In other words, from the first course to the last.

From soup to nuts
–Popular saying.

The whole hog
–Popular saying.

 ## Multis enim serviet, qui corpori servit.

One who serves his body will serve many masters.
–Seneca, *EM* 14.1.

The glutton digs his grave with his teeth.
–English proverb.

Drink

🏛 ἐμοὶ δὲ μόνοις πρόπινε τοῖς ὄμμασιν.

Drink to me only with your eyes.

> –Philostratus the Elder, *Ep.* 33, in a
> letter to an unnamed woman whose
> beautiful eyes he compares with
> goblets of silver and gold. "Put the
> cups down," he says "and drink to me
> only with your eyes."

Drink to me only with thine eyes, and I will
pledge with mine.

> –Ben Jonson, "Song: To Celia" (1616).

🏛 κάτοπτρον εἴδους χαλκός ἐστ', οἶνος
δὲ νοῦ.

Bronze is the mirror of one's shape, wine of one's mind.

> –Aeschylus, frag. 393. Ancient mirrors
> were made of polished bronze.

οἶνος γὰρ ἀνθρώπῳ δίοπτρον.

Wine is a peephole into a man.

> –Alcaeus, frag. 333.

ἀμαθίην γὰρ ἄμεινον κρύπτειν ἔργον δὲ
ἐν ἀνέσει καὶ παρ' οἶνον.

*It's better to hide lack of knowledge, but this is hard when at
leisure and drinking wine.*

> –Heraclitus, quoted in Plutarch, *Q Conv.*
> 644f (= frag. 95, D-K).

Wine in, truth out

> –Charles Dickens, *Nicholas Nickleby*, ch.
> 27 (1839).

In vino veritas (In wine, truth)

> –Now a popular saying, its source being Erasmus's *Adages*. Pliny the Elder 14.142 comes close with "Volgoque veritas iam attributa vino est" (Truth is commonly attributed to wine).

🏛 διὸ καὶ καλῶς οἱ παροιμιαζόμενοι λέγουσι τὸν οἶνον οὐκ ἔχειν πηδάλια.

Those who cite proverbs say well that wine has no rudder.

> –Phocylides, frag. 14, quoted in Athenaeus 10.427f.

First you take a drink, then the drink takes a drink, then the drink takes you.

> –F. Scott Fitzgerald, attributed.

🏛 **Inter pocula**

Among their cups.

> –Persius 1.30. Persius is decrying the state of poetry in his day and says that Romans at banquets, when "inter pocula," long to fawn on the poets performing, no matter how bad they are.

In his/her/their cups.

> –Popular saying, now conveying the idea that someone is drunk.

🏛 **Sine Cerere et Libero friget Venus.**

Without Ceres and Bacchus, Venus grows cold.

> –Terence, *Eun.* 732. Ceres was the god of grain and Liber/Bacchus of wine.

One more drink and I'd have been under the
host.

–Dorothy Parker, quoted in Bennett Cerf,
Try and Stop Me (1944).

🏛 ἐνῆν ἄρ', ὡς ἔοικε, κἀν οἴνῳ λόγος·
ἔνιοι δ' ὕδωρ πίνοντές εἰσ'
ἀβέλτεροι.

*There is, so it seems, thoughtfulness in wine as well, and some
water drinkers are empty headed.*

–Amphis, quoted in Athenaeus 2.44a.

Nulla placere diu nec vivere carmina possunt / quae scribuntur aquae potoribus.

*Poems that are written by water drinkers can neither please nor
live a long time.*

–Horace, *Epist.* 1.19.2.

I wish some of you would tell me the brand of
whiskey that Grant drinks. I would like to
send a barrel of it to my other generals.

–Abraham Lincoln, attributed,
responding to complaints about
Ulysses S. Grant's drinking.

Teaching has ruined more American novelists
than drink.

–Gore Vidal, *Oui* magazine (April, 1975).

Forgiveness

🏛 σύγγνωθ'· ἁμαρτεῖν εἰκὸς ἀνθρώπους,
τέκνον.

Be forgiving! It is natural for humans to err, son.
−Euripides, *Hipp.* 615.

To err is human, to forgive, divine.
−Popular saying, originally from
Alexander Pope, "An Essay on
Criticism" (1711).

🏛 **Multa ignoscendo fit potens
potentior.**

By forgiving much a powerful man becomes more powerful.
−Publilius Syrus 391.

I have always found that mercy bears richer
fruits than strict justice.
−Abraham Lincoln, attributed.

🏛 **Ignoscito saepe alteri; nunquam tibi.**

Always forgive the other fellow, never yourself.
−Publilius Syrus, in some collections.

Ignoscas aliis multa: nihil tibi.

You should forgive much in others, nothing in yourself.
−Cleobulus, quoted in Ausonius, *App.*
3.16.

To be one's own worst critic
−Popular saying.

🏛 ## Hoc denique tibi circa mortis diem praesta: moriantur ante te vitia.

Finally, see to this concerning the day of your death—let your faults die before you do.

> –Seneca, *EM* 27.2.

Every day in every way I'm getting a little better.

> –Popular saying, originally from Émile Coué, a nineteenth-century proponent of self-improvement techniques.

🏛 ## Omnia enim vitia in aperto leniora sunt.

All flaws are milder out in the open.

> –Seneca, *EM* 56.10.

To air one's dirty linen

> –Popular saying.

🏛 ## Suus cuique attributus est error: / sed non videmus manticae quod in tergost.

Each person is endowed with his own flaw, but we do not see the part of the bag that is on our back.

> –Catullus 22.20–21. Another version in Phaedrus 4.10 expands this thought.

In other men we faults can spy, / and blame the mote that dims their eye; / each little speck and blemish find, / to our own stronger errors blind.

> –John Gay, "The Turkey and the Ant," *The Fables* (1727).

Friends & Enemies

 Amici vitia si feras, facias tua.
If you tolerate the faults of a friend, you make them yours.
–Publilius Syrus 10.

'Tis great Confidence in a Friend to tell him
your Faults, greater to tell him his.
–Benjamin Franklin, *Poor Richard's*
Almanack (1751).

 "κολοιός" φασι "παρὰ κολοιὸν ἰζάνει."
As people say, jackdaw sits down with jackdaw.
–Aristotle, *Mag. Mor.* 1208b.

**τέττιξ μὲν τέττιγι φίλος, μύρμακι δὲ
μύρμαξ, / ἵρακες δ' ἵραξιν.**
*Cicada is friends with a cicada, ant with ant, hawks with
hawks.*
–Theocritus, *Id.* 9.31–32.

**Pares autem, vetere proverbio, cum
paribus facillime congregantur.**
*Now equals, according to the old proverb, most readily
associate with equals.*
–Cicero, *Sen.* 6.

Birds of a feather flock together.
–Popular saying.

🏛 ## Amicus certus in re incerta cernitur.

A true friend is seen when times are tough.

—Ennius, frag. 166, quoted in Cicero,
Amic. 64.

ἐν τοῖς κακοῖς γὰρ ἀγαθοὶ σαφέστατοι / φίλοι.

Good friends are most clearly visible in hard times.

—Euripides, *Hec.* 1226–27.

Nihil agit qui diffidentem verbis solatur suis; / is est amicus, qui in dubia re iuvat, ubi re est opus.

*One who comforts an anxious friend with his words does
nothing. That one is a friend who helps in a tight spot
when there is need of action.*

—Plautus, *Epid.* 111.

δοκίμαζε τοὺς φίλους ἔκ τε τῆς περὶ τὸν βίον ἀτυχίας καὶ τῆς ἐν τοῖς κινδύνοις κοινωνίας.

*Judge your friends by the misfortune surrounding your life
and their sharing in dangers.*

—Isocrates, *Dem.* 25.

A friend in need is a friend indeed.

—Popular saying.

🏛 ## Servandus ergo est omni diligentia raro inventus amicus, est enim alter ego.

*That rarely found friend must be preserved with all diligence,
for he is another I.*

—Pseudo-Seneca, *Mor.* 20.

ἄλλος ἐγώ

Another I

> –Zeno, quoted in Diogenes Laertius
> 7.1.23.

ὁ φίλος ἕτερος ἐγώ.

A friend is another self.

> –Aristotle, *Mag. Mor.* 1213a.24.

Amicus . . . est tamquam alter idem.

A friend . . . is like another self.

> –Cicero, *Amic.* 80.

Idem velle atque idem nolle, ea demum firma amicitia est.

To be for and against the same thing—in the end this is a solid friendship.

> –Sallust, *Cat.* 20.4.

Two lovely berries moulded on one stem: / so, with two seeming bodies, but one heart.

> –William Shakespeare, *A Midsummer Night's Dream*, act 3 scene 2 (1595).

🏛 Cum fortuna manet, vultum servatis amici.

As long as good luck abides, you can count on seeing the face of a friend.

> –Petronius 80.

Qui amicus esse coepit, quia expedit, et desinet, quia expedit.

Someone who starts being your friend because it's to his benefit will also stop being your friend because it's to his benefit.

> –Seneca, *EM* 9.9

Donec eris sospes multos numerabis amicos: / tempora si fuerint nubila, solus eris.

As long as you remain lucky you will count many friends; if the weather turn cloudy, you'll be alone.

–Ovid, *Tr.* 1.9.5–6.

Fair-weather friends

–Popular saying.

Friendship, n. A ship big enough to carry two in fair weather, but only one in foul.

–Ambrose Bierce, *The Devil's Dictionary* (1911).

🏛 Saepe ex / malo principio magna familiaritas conflatast.

Often a great friendship has been formed from a bad beginning.

–Terence, *Eun.* 873–74.

Louis, I think this is the beginning of a beautiful friendship.

–Spoken by Humphrey Bogart playing Rick Blaine in *Casablanca*, film (1942); last line of the film. Screenplay by Julius Epstein, Philip Epstein, and Howard Koch.

🏛 Verae amicitiae sempiternae sunt.

True friendships are forever.

–Cicero, *Amic.* 32.

If you live to be a hundred, I want to live to be a
hundred minus one day, so I never have to live
without you.

–A. A. Milne, *The House at Pooh Corner*
(1928), attributed falsely.

🏛 ## Vulgare amici nomen, sed rara est fides.

The title of friend is common, but loyalty is rare.
–Phaedrus 3.9.1.

True friendship is a plant of slow growth, and
must undergo and withstand the shocks
of adversity before it is entitled to the
appellation.

–George Washington, letter to Bushrod
Washington (January 15, 1783).

🏛 ## τὸ μὲν γὰρ χρυσίον ἐν τῷ πυρὶ βασανίζομεν, τοὺς δὲ φίλους ἐν ταῖς ἀτυχίαις διαγιγνώσκομεν.

*We test gold in fire and likewise we test friends in times of
difficulty.*
–Isocrates, *Dem.* 25.

The firmest friendships have been formed in
mutual adversity, as iron is most strongly
united by the fiercest flame.

–Charles Caleb Colton, *Lacon* (1825).

De inimico non loquaris male sed cogites.

You shouldn't speak ill of your enemy, but you can think about it.

–Publilius Syrus 150.

Don't get mad, get even.

–Popular saying.

Don't get mad, get everything.

–Spoken by Ivana Trump playing herself in *The First Wives Club*, film (1996). Screenplay by Robert Harling.

Iratum breviter vites, inimicum diu.

You should avoid an angry man for a while, an enemy for a long time.

–Publilius Syrus 288.

Keep your friends close, but your enemies closer.

–Spoken by Al Pacino playing Michael Corleone in *The Godfather Part II* (1974). Screenplay by Francis Ford Coppola and Mario Puzo.

Nihil inimicius quam sibi ipse.

Nothing is more hostile than he is to himself.

–Cicero, *Att.* 205.3.

He's his own worst enemy.

–Popular saying.

Latet anguis in herba.

A snake lurks in the grass.

–Vergil, *Ecl.* 3.93.

Snake in the grass

–Popular saying.

 ὄξος τ᾽ ἄλειφά τ᾽ ἐγχέας ταὐτῷ κύτει / διχοστατοῦντ᾽ ἂν οὐ φίλω προσεννέποις.

Pour vinegar and oil into the same bowl. They'll stay apart and you could hardly call them friends.

–Aeschylus, *Ag.* 322–23.

They're like oil and vinegar.

–Popular saying.

Fight like cats and dogs

–Popular saying.

 ὁ φίλος τῷ φίλῳ βούλεται τἀγαθὰ ἐκείνου ἕνεκα.

A friend wishes good things for his friend, for that one's sake.

–Aristotle, *Eth. Nic.* 1159a.

The only reward of virtue is virtue; the only way to have a friend is to be one.

–Ralph Waldo Emerson, "Friendship," *Essays* (1841).

Futility

🏛 τίς γλαῦκ' Ἀθήναζ' ἤγαγεν;

Who brought an owl to Athens?

> –Aristophanes, *Av.* 301. As Athena's
> animal, owls abounded in Athens,
> inhabiting the Acropolis and
> appearing on Athenian coins. Cicero
> liked the saying (*Fam.* 176.2 and
> 243.4).

In silvam non ligna feras.

Don't bring wood into the forest.

> –Horace, *Sat.* 1.10.34.

Quis mel Aristaeo, quis Baccho vina Falerna, / Triptolemo fruges, poma det Alcinoo?

Who would give honey to Aristaeus, Falernian wine to Bacchus, grain to Triptolemus, or fruit to Alcinous?

> –Ovid, *Pont.* 4.2.9–10. Often simplified
> to "Alcimoo poma dare." Aristaeus
> invented beekeeping, Triptolemus
> spread the art of agriculture, Alcinous
> owned famous gardens, and Bacchus
> was the god of wine and fertility. See a
> similar sentiment in Martial 7.41.

Bringing coals to Newcastle

> –Popular saying.

καθ' ὕδατος, φασὶν, γράφεις.

As the saying goes, you are writing on water.

–Lucian, *Catapl.* 21.

Piscari in aere / et venari in medio mari

To go fishing in the air and hunting in the middle of the sea

–Plautus, *Asin.* 99–100.

Tilting at windmills

–Popular saying, indicating pursuit
of unattainable goals. The idea is
traceable to the story of Don Quixote.

 ἐς τὸν Δαναΐδων πίθον ὑδροφορήσειν
μοι δοκῶ.

I seem to be carrying water in the Danaids' jar.

–Lucian, *Tim.* 18. For killing their
husbands, the fifty daughters of
Danaus were condemned to Tartarus,
where they forever carried water in
perforated jars.

I pray thee, cease thy counsel, / which falls into
mine ears as profitless / as water in a sieve.

–William Shakespeare, *Much Ado About
Nothing*, act 5 scene 1 (1598–99).

Insanus medio flumine quaeris aquam!

You idiot! You're looking for water in the middle of the river.

–Propertius 1.9.16.

You can't see what's right under your nose.

–Popular saying.

🏛 **In pertusum ingerimus dicta dolium, operam ludimus.**

We're pouring our words into a broken jar, wasting our time.

–Plautus, *Pseud.* 369.

We're just spinning our wheels.

–Popular saying.

🏛 τά σῦκα ταῖς σφενδόναις τρυγᾶσθαι

To harvest figs with slings

–Plutarch, *De exil.* 602b, quoting an unnamed comic writer.

It's like trying to nail Jello to a wall.

–Popular saying.

Golden Rule

 ἃ πάσχοντες ὑφ' ἑτέρων ὀργίζεσθε,
ταῦτα τοὺς ἄλλους μὴ ποιεῖτε.

*Don't do to others the things you get angry at when they are
done to you by others.*

–Isocrates, *Nic.* 61.

τοιοῦτος γίγνου περὶ τοὺς γονεῖς, οἵους
ἂν εὔξαιο περὶ σεαυτὸν γενέσθαι τοὺς
σεαυτοῦ παῖδας.

*Be toward your parents the way you would want your
children to be to you.*

–Isocrates, *Dem.* 14.

Quod tibi fieri non vis, alteri ne feceris.

*Don't do to someone else that which you don't want done to
yourself.*

–Emperor Severus Alexander, quoted in
SHA, Sev. 51.7.

Do not do unto others as you would that they
should do unto you. Their tastes may not be
the same.

–George Bernard Shaw, *Man and
Superman, Maxims for Revolutionists*
(1903); cf. "Do unto others as you
would have them do unto you" (Matt.
7:12).

Good & Evil

🏛 **Peccare pauci nolunt, nulli nesciunt.**
A few are unwilling to do wrong, no one doesn't know how.
–Publilius Syrus 532.

Adam was but human—this explains it all. He
did not want the apple for the apple's sake, he
wanted it only because it was forbidden. The
mistake was in not forbidding the serpent;
then he would have eaten the serpent.
–Mark Twain, epigraph to ch. 2,
Pudd'nhead Wilson (1867).

🏛 **Nocere posse et nolle laus
amplissima est.**
*To be able to do harm and be unwilling to do so is the highest
praise.*
–Publilius Syrus 442.

I think I did something for the worst possible
reason—just because I could. I think that's
the most, just about the most morally
indefensible reason that anybody could have
for doing anything.
–Bill Clinton, interview on *60 Minutes*,
discussing his affair with Monica
Lewinsky (June 20, 2004).

Lupus est homo homini.

People treat each other like wolves.

–Plautus, *Asin.* 495.

If God lived on earth, people would break His windows!

–Spoken by Molly Picon playing Yente
in *Fiddler on the Roof,* film (1971).
Screenplay by Joseph Stein.

Gossip

🏛 **Fama, malum qua non aliud velocius ullum.**

Gossip! No other evil thing is faster than it is.

–Vergil, *Aen.* 4.174.

Nihil est autem tam volucre, quam maledictum; nihil facilius emittitur; nihil citius excipitur, nihil latius dissipatur.

Nothing flies faster than slander; nothing is sent forth so easily, nothing is received more quickly, nothing spreads further.

–Cicero, *Planc.* 57.

Gossip needs no carriage.

–Russian proverb.

🏛 οὐδὲν γὰρ οὕτως ἐστιν ἀνθρώποις γλυκύ ὡς τοὐκλαλεῖν τἀλλότρια.

Nothing is sweeter for folks than to talk away about other folks' affairs.

–Menander, frag. 496 (*FCG*).

μὴ . . . χελιδόνας ἐν οἰκίᾳ δέχεσθαι.

Don't welcome swallows under your roof.

–Plutarch, *Symp.* 727c. Swallows were known as chatterers in antiquity and, Plutarch suggests, were potential gossips. Plutarch is quoting Pythagoras.

A little bird told me.
> –Popular saying.

🏛 ## Absentes tinnitu aurium praesentire sermones de se receptum est.

It is generally accepted that people who are absent can sense by a ringing in the ears when they are being talked about.
> –Pliny the Elder 28.24.

If your ears are ringing, someone's talking about you.
> –Popular saying.

If your right ear itches, someone is speaking well of you, and if your left ear itches, someone is speaking ill of you.
> –Popular saying.

🏛 ## ξίφος τιτρώσκει σῶμα, τὸν δὲ νοῦν λόγος.

A sword wounds the body, words the mind.
> –Menander, *Mon.* 393.

Sticks and stones will break my bones, but words will never hurt me.
> –Popular saying.

Gratitude (See also Charity)

🏛 **[Noli] dentes inspicere equi donati.**
Don't inspect the teeth of a horse given as a gift.

> –St. Jerome, *Commentary on Paul's Epistle
> to the Ephesians*, prologue. Jerome says
> the phrase is a *vulgare proverbium,* a
> common proverb.

Don't look a gift horse in the mouth.
> –Popular saying.

Don't bite the hand that feeds you.
> –Popular saying.

Gullibility

🏛 ## Fere libenter homines id quod volunt credunt.

People quite readily believe what they wish for.

–Julius Caesar, *B Gall.* 3.18.

There's a sucker born every minute.

–P. T. Barnum, attributed.

🏛 ## Quod nimis miseri volunt, hoc facile credunt.

What miserable people want the most is what they readily believe.

–Seneca, *Herc. F.* 313.

Grasping at straws

–Popular saying.

Habit

 οὐδὲ γὰρ κύων ἅπαξ παύσαιτ' ἂν
σκυτοραγεῖν μαθοῦσα.

*Having learned to chew on our shoes once, a dog will never
stop.*

> –Lucian, *Ind.* 25–26.

Ut canis a corio nunquam absterrebitur uncto

Like a dog that can never be scared off a bit of oiled leather

> –Horace, *Sat.* 2.5.83.

Old habits die hard.

> –Popular saying.

 Sumuntur a conversantibus mores.

Habits are acquired from those with whom we keep company.

> –Seneca, *Ira* 3.8.1.

A man is known by the company he keeps.

> –Popular saying.

Happy & Sad

🏛 **Nihil est ab omni / parte beatum.**
Nothing is entirely fortunate.
–Horace, *Carm.* 2.16.27–28.

A mixed blessing
–Popular saying.

🏛 **Tum mos erat in adversis rebus voltum secundae fortunae gerere, moderari animo in secundis.**
It was the custom then to wear the face of good fortune in hard times but to control your spirit in good times.
–Livy 43.62.11.

Gray skies are gonna clear up, put on a happy face.
–Charles Strouse, "Put on a Happy Face," song in *Bye Bye Birdie* (1960).

🏛 **Felix est non qui aliis videtur sed qui sibi.**
He is happy who seems that way not to others but to himself.
–Pseudo-Seneca, *Rem.* 16.9.

And perhaps that's why—no, I'm sure that's the reason why—I think of myself as happy on the inside and other people think I'm happy on the outside.
–Anne Frank, *Diary of a Young Girl*, entry for August 1, 1944 (1947).

🏛 ## Tam miser est quisque quam credidit.

Each person is as unhappy as he has come to believe he is.
   –Seneca, *EM* 78.12.

Happiness, to some elation; / is to others, mere stagnation.
   –Amy Lowell, "Happiness," *Sword Blades and Poppy Seed* (1914).

🏛 ## Quid rides? Mutato nomine de te / fabula narratur.

What are you laughing about? Change the name and the story is about you.
   –Horace, *Sat.* 1.1.69–70.

Everything is funny as long as it is happening to somebody else.
   –Will Rogers, *The Illiterate Digest* (1924).

🏛 ## ἐκ τοῦ παθεῖν γίγνωσκε καὶ τὸ συμπαθεῖν.

From suffering learn to suffer along with someone else.
   –Philemon, frag. 51b (*FCG*).

Human beings, who are almost unique in having the ability to learn from the experience of others, are also remarkable for their apparent disinclination to do so.
   –Douglas Adams, *Last Chance to See* (1990).

🏛 Interdum lacrimae pondera vocis
 habent.

Sometimes tears have the weight of speech.
–Ovid, *Pont.* 3.1.158.

Sweet tears! The awful language, eloquent of
infinite affection; far too big for words.
–Robert Pollok, *The Course of Time*
(1827).

🏛 Paratae lacrimae insidias non fletum
 indicant

Prepared tears indicate a trap, not weeping.
–Publilius Syrus 536.

Ille dolet vere qui sine teste dolet.

He grieves truly who grieves without a witness.
–Martial, *Epig.* 1.33.4.

Crocodile tears
–Popular saying, based on an ancient
belief that crocodiles shed false tears
before eating a human.

If that the earth could teem with woman's tears,
/ each drop she falls would prove a crocodile.
–William Shakespeare, *Othello*, act 4
scene 1 (1603–4).

🏛 χρόνος μαλάξει, νῦν δ' ἔθ' ἡβάσκει,
 κακόν.

Time will soften the pain even though it is now flourishing.
–Euripides, *Alc.* 1085.

πάντων ἰατρὸς ἀναγκαίων κακῶν /
χρόνος ἐστῖν.

Time is the doctor for all unavoidable evils.

—Menander, frag. 131 (*FCG*).

Nihil non aut lenit aut domat diuturnitas.

*There is nothing that a length of time will not either soothe
or overcome.*

—Publilius Syrus 467.

Etiam sanato vulnere cicatrix manet.

Even after the wound has healed, the scar remains.

—Publilius Syrus, in some collections.

Tempus fecit aerumnas leves.

Time made the troubles light.

—Seneca, *Thy.* 305.

Nullus dolor est quem non longinquitas
temporis minuat ac molliat.

*There is no sorrow that length of time will not diminish and
soften.*

—Cicero, *Fam.* 244.3. Servius Sulpicius
writing to Cicero on the death of
Cicero's daughter, Tullia.

Time heals all wounds.

—Popular saying.

🏛 ## Quid iuvat dolori suo occurrere?

What's gained by running out to meet one's sorrow?

—Seneca, *EM* 13.10.

Why borrow trouble?

—Popular saying.

Haste

🏛 Sat celeriter fieri, quidquid fiat satis bene.

Whatever is done well enough is done quickly enough.

> –Augustus, quoted in Suetonius, *Aug.* 25.4, claiming it was one of Augustus's favorite sayings.

σπεῦδε βραδέως.

Make haste—slowly.

> –Augustus, quoted in Suetonius, *Aug.* 25.4. Suetonius gives the Greek, apparently quoting Augustus directly. The Latin version, "Festina lente," was popularized in Erasmus, *Adages* 2.11.

Wisely and slow. They stumble that run fast.

> –William Shakespeare, *Romeo and Juliet*, act 2 scene 3 (1595).

🏛 Omnia non properanti clara certaque erunt; festinatio improvida est et caeca.

All things will be clear and certain for one not in a hurry; haste is rash and blind.

> –Livy 22.39.22.

Haste makes waste.

> –Popular saying.

🏛 ## Nusquam est qui ubique est.

He is nowhere who is everywhere.
> –Seneca, *EM* 2.2.

He's all over the place.
> –Popular saying.

🏛 ## Ad paenitendum properat, cito qui iudicat.

Who judges in haste, rushes to repentance.
> –Publilius Syrus 32.

In iudicando criminosa est celeritas.

Haste in judging is a crime.
> –Publilius Syrus 293.

Velox consilium sequitur poenitentia.

Repentance follows a plan made in haste.
> –Publilius Syrus 734.

Decide not rashly. The decision made / can never be recalled.
> –Henry Wadsworth Longfellow, "Masque of Pandora: III. Tower of Prometheus on Mount Caucasus" (1875).

🏛 ## Ne frena animo permitte calenti. / Da spatium, tenuemque moram. Male cuncta ministrat / impetus.

Don't give the reins to a heated mind. Give it space and a brief delay. Haste serves all things poorly.
> –Statius, *Theb.* 10.703–5.

Deliberation, n. The act of examining one's bread to determine which side it is buttered on.
–Ambrose Bierce, *The Devil's Dictionary* (1911).

History

🏛 **Nescire autem quid antea quam natus sis acciderit, id est semper esse puerum.**

Not to know what happened before you were born is always to be a child.

—Cicero, *Orat.* 120.

Those who cannot remember the past are condemned to repeat it.

—George Santayana, *The Life of Reason: The Phases of Human Progress*, vol. 1, *Reason in Common Sense* (1905–6).

A generation which ignores history has no past—and no future.

—Robert Heinlein, *Time Enough for Love* (1973).

🏛 **Quid vero historiae de nobis ad annos DC praedicarint?**

What will history have to say about me six hundred years from now?

—Cicero, *Att.* 25.1.

Reputation is an idle / and most false imposition; oft got without merit, and lost / without deserving.

—William Shakespeare, *Othello*, act 2 scene 3 (1603–4).

🏛 ἱστορία φιλοσοφία ἐστὶν ἐκ
παραδειγμάτων.

History is philosophy based on examples.

–Pseudo-Dionysius of Halicarnassus,
Rhet. 11.2, paraphrasing Thucydides
2.22.

History is philosophy teaching by example, and
also warning; its two eyes are geography and
chronology.

–James A. Garfield, attributed, apparently
falsely.

Home & Away

🏛 ὡς οὐδὲν γλύκιον ἧς πατρίδος οὐδὲ
τοκήων γίγνεται.

*So it is that nothing is sweeter in the end than country and
parents.*

> –Homer, *Od.* 9.34–35.

οἴκοι βέλτερον εἶναι.

It's better at home.

> –Hesiod, *Op.* 365.

Quae est domestica sede iucundior?

What place is more pleasant than the site of one's home?

> –Cicero, *Fam.* 229.2.

There's no place like home.

> –Spoken by Judy Garland playing
> Dorothy, *The Wizard of Oz*, film
> (1939). Screenplay by Noel Langley,
> Florence Ryerson, and Edgar Allan
> Woolf.

🏛 **Non convalescit planta quae saepe
transfertur.**

A plant that is often relocated does not grow strong.

> –Seneca, *EM* 2.3.

Stay, stay at home, my heart, and rest; / home-
keeping hearts are happiest.

> –Henry Wadsworth Longfellow, "Song"
> (1826).

Nec domo dominus, sed domino domus honestanda est.

The owner should ennoble the house, not the house the owner.
–Cicero, *Off.* 1.139.

Although very few people are actually called upon to live in palaces, a very large number are unwilling to admit the fact.

–Osbert Lancaster, *Homes Sweet Homes* (1939).

 Dulcius urbe quid est?

What is sweeter than the city?

–Sulpicia 14.3. Sulpicia bemoans the fact that she has to go to the country for her birthday, leaving her beloved Cerinthus behind in Rome.

Rus in urbe est.

[Your] country is in the city.

–Martial, *Epig.* 12.57.21, praising a friend's house that is so situated and arranged as to offer the peace of the country while being situated in Rome itself.

There is nothing good to be had in the country, or if there is, they will not let you have it.

–William Hazlitt, "Observations on Mr. Wordsworth's Poem, 'The Excursion,'" *The Round Table* (1817).

Honesty

🏛 Quod sentimus loquamur, quod loquimur sentiamus.

Let's say what we feel and feel what we say.
    –Seneca, *EM* 75.4.

I meant what I said, and I said what I meant. /
An elephant's faithful, one hundred percent.
    –Dr. Seuss, *Horton Hatches the Egg*
    (1940).

🏛 **Esse, quam videri, bonus malebat.**

As a good person, he wished to be good more than to appear to be good.
    –Sallust, *Cat.* 54.6, speaking about Cato
    the Younger; cf. Plato, *Resp.* 361b and
    the state motto of North Carolina,
    "Esse quam videri."

Things are seldom what they seem, skim milk masquerades as cream.
    –W. S. Gilbert and Arthur Sullivan,
    "Things Are Seldom as They Seem,"
    song in *HMS Pinafore* (1878).

Hope

 αἱ δ᾽ ἐλπίδες βόσκουσι φυγάδας, ὡς λόγος.

Hopes feed fugitives, as the saying goes.

–Euripides, *Phoen.* 396.

Extreme hopes are born of extreme misery.

–Bertrand Russell, "The Future of
Mankind," *Unpopular Essays* (1950).

 Una salus victis, nullam sperare salutem.

There is a single salvation for the conquered, not to hope for salvation.

–Vergil, *Aen.* 2.354.

In War: Resolution. In Defeat: Defiance. In Victory: Magnanimity. In Peace: Good Will.

–Winston Churchill, *The Second World War*, vol. 1, *The Gathering Storm* (1948). Churchill said this was the moral of his book.

 θαρσεῖν χρή, φίλε Βάττε· ταχ᾽ αὔριον ἔσσετ᾽ ἄμεινον.

You must take courage, dear Battus! Tomorrow will be soon better.

–Theocritus, *Id.* 4.41.

I'll think of it tomorrow, at Tara. I can stand
it then. Tomorrow, I'll think of some way
to get him back. After all, tomorrow is
another day.

> –Margaret Mitchell, *Gone with the Wind*,
> ch. 63 (1936); last lines of the book
> and the film (1939) of the same name.

🏛 Aegroto, dum anima est spes esse dicitur.

*As the saying goes, as long as there is breath in a sick person,
there is hope.*

> –Cicero, *Att.* 177.3.

Where there's life, there's hope.

> –Popular saying.

Human Nature

 ὁ ἄνθρωπος εὐεργετικὸς πεφυκώς.

Man is born as one who is a doer of good.

–Marcus Aurelius 9.42.5.

Because I still believe, in spite of everything,
that people are truly good at heart.

–Anne Frank, *Diary of a Young Girl*, entry
for July 15, 1944 (1947).

 οὔποτε ποιήσεις τὸν κάρκινον ὀρθὰ
βαδίζειν.

You'll never get a crab to walk upright.

–Aristophanes, *Pax* 1083.

Vulpes pilum mutat, non mores.

A fox changes its pelt, not its habits.

–Vespasian, quoted in Suetonius, *Vesp.*
16.3.

Colubra restem non parit.

A snake doesn't give birth to rope.

–Petronius 45.

Naturam mutare difficile est.

It is difficult to change one's nature.

–Seneca, *Ira* 2.20.2.

A leopard doesn't change its spots.

–Popular saying.

Human action can be modified to some extent,
but human nature cannot be changed.

> –Abraham Lincoln, speech at Cooper
> Union (February 27, 1860).

⛪ Mala mens, malus animus

Bad mind, bad spirit

> –Terence, *An.* 164.

Bad to the bone

> –Popular saying.

⛪ Etiam illud adiungo, saepius ad laudem atque virtutem naturam sine doctrina, quam sine natura valuisse doctrinam.

*I add this as well—nature without study leads more often to
praise and virtue than does study without nature.*

> –Cicero, *Arch.* 15.

Nature vs. nurture

> –Common phrase concerning the
> debate over the power of genetics vs.
> environment.

⛪ Homo sum; humani nihil a me alienum puto.

I'm human and I think that nothing human is alien to me.

> –Terence, *Heaut.* 77.

Dum inter homines sumus, colamus humanitatem.

So long as we are among men, let us cultivate humanity.
–Seneca, *Ira* 4.43.5.

ἄνθρωπον ὄντα δεῖ φρονεῖν τἀνθρώπινα.

Being human, one should think about human things.
–Menander, *Mon.* 1.

Know then thyself, presume not God to scan; /
the proper study of mankind is man.
–Alexander Pope, "An Essay on Man:
Epistle II," *Moral Essays* (1733–34).

🏛 **οὕτω δὲ καὶ τὰ μὲν δίκαια πράττοντες δίκαιοι γινόμεθα, τὰ δὲ σώφρονα σώφρονες, τὰ δ' ἀνδρεῖα ἀνδρεῖοι.**

Thus it is. We become just by doing just things, prudent by doing prudent things, and brave by doing brave things.
–Aristotle, *Eth. Nic.* 1103b.

Our deeds determine us, as much as we determine our deeds.
–George Eliot, *Adam Bede* (1859).

Hypocrisy

🏛 **Est enim proprium stultitiae aliorum vitia cernere, oblivisci suorum.**

It is a sign of foolishness to take note of the flaws in others but to be unaware of one's own.

–Cicero, *Tusc.* 3.73.

Aliena vitia in oculis habemus, a tergo nostra sunt.

We have others' vices before our eyes; our own are behind our backs.

–Seneca, *Ira* 2.28.8.

Peras imposuit Jupiter nobis duas: / propriis repletam vitiis post tergum dedit. / Alienis ante pectus suspendit gravem. / Hac re videre nostra mala non possumus; / alii simul delinquunt, censores sumus.

Jupiter has placed two sacks on us. He gave us one on our back filled with our own flaws and hung the one heavy with those of others in front of our chest. That way we can't see our own misdeeds, but as soon as others slip, we are censors.

–Phaedrus 4.10.1–5. *Censor* can mean
simply a severe judge or can refer to
Roman governmental officials charged
with oversight of public morality.

Nothing so needs reforming as other people's habits.

–Mark Twain, *Pudd'nhead Wilson,*
epigraph to ch. 15 (1894).

Indecision

 "ἀλλ' ἔγωγε," ἔφη "ἀπὸ τοῦ νῦν ἀποτάσσομαί σου τῆς φιλίας, ὅτι ἐκ τοῦ αὐτοῦ στόματος τὸ θερμὸ καὶ τὸ ψυχρὸν ἐξάγεις."

"But," he said, "from now I say goodbye to you as a friend, because out of the same mouth you produce both hot and cold."

–Aesop, "The Satyr and the Traveler" (Perry 35).

"Nolo" ait "ut nostris umquam successerit antris, tam diversa duo qui simul ora ferat."

"I do not want," he said, "anyone ever to come near my cave who carries about two things in his mouth at once."

–Avianus 29. In both stories, the satyr had welcomed a traveler who both blew on his hands to warm them and on his food to cool it.

To blow hot and cold

–Popular saying.

 Duo insequens lepores neutrum capit.

Who follows two hares captures neither.

–Erasmus, *Adages* 5.2236, giving this as the Latin translation of an unattributed Greek proverb, ὁ δύο πτῶκας διώκων οὐδέτερον καταλαμβάνει.

Quo caveas, cum animus aliud verba aliud petunt?

How can you be cautious when your mind wants one thing and your words another?

–Publilius Syrus 615.

When You Come to a Fork in the Road, Take It!

–Yogi Berra, title of book (2001).

Industry

🏛 **Faber est suae quisque fortunae.**

Everyone is the craftsman of his own fortune.

> –Appius Claudius Caecus, quoted in
> Pseudo-Sallust, *Ad Caes. sen.* 1.1.
> Often recast as, "Est unus quisque
> faber ipse fortunae suae."

God gives all things to industry.

> –Benjamin Franklin, *Poor Richard's
> Almanack* (1758).

Life is what you make of it.

> –Popular saying and title of several
> songs.

🏛 **Homo ad duas res, ad intelligendum
et ad agendum, est natus.**

Mankind was born for two things—thinking and doing.

> –Cicero, *Fin.* 2.40, quoting Aristotle;
> commonly misquoted and
> condensed into "Facta non verba."

The way to get started is to quit talking and
begin doing.

> –Walt Disney, attributed.

🏛 **Iucundi acti labores.**

Completed labors are pleasant.

> –Cicero, *Fin.* 2.105, citing it as a
> common saying.

Now is done thy long day's work. / Fold thy palms across thy breast, / fold thine arms, turn to thy rest.

–Alfred Tennyson, "A Dirge" (1830).

Justice

 νικᾷ δ' ὁ μειών τὸν μέγαν, δίκαι' ἔχων.

The lesser overcomes the greater as long as it possesses what is just.

–Euripides, *Supp.* 437.

ὀψὲ θεῶν ἀλέουσι μύλοι, ἀλέουσι δὲ λεπτά.

The mills of the gods grind late, but they grind fine.

–Sextus Empiricus, *Against the Professors* 1.287. Plutarch, in *De sera* 549d, discusses the validity of the proverb.

Though the mills of God grind slowly, / yet they grind exceeding small; / though with patience he stands waiting, / with exactness grinds he all.

–Henry Wadsworth Longfellow, translation of Friedrich von Logau, "Retribution," *Sinngedichte* 3.2.24 (ca. 1654).

 Nocens habuit aliquando latendi fortunam, numquam fiduciam.

A guilty person sometimes has the good fortune to avoid detection, but never has any faith that it will happen.

–Seneca, *EM* 105.8.

Always looking over your shoulder

–Popular saying.

🏛 "ἄκουε δή," ἦ δ' ὅς. "φημὶ γὰρ ἐγὼ εἶναι τὸ δίκαιον οὐκ ἄλλο τι ἢ τὸ τοῦ κρείττονος συμφέρον."

"Well listen," he said, "I say that justice is simply the advantage of the stronger."

> –Plato, *Resp.* 344c, Thrasymachus speaking to Socrates.

δίκαιος ἀνὴρ ἀδίκου πανταχοῦ ἔλαττον ἔχει.

The just man always comes out worse than the unjust one.

> –Plato, Resp. 343d, Thrasymachus speaking to Socrates.

Mensuraque iuris / vis erat.

The measure of what was right was power.

> –Lucan 1.175–76, describing a low point in Roman history.

Ius est in armis.

Right exists in force of arms.

> –Seneca, *Herc. F.* 253.

Might makes right.

> –Popular saying.

Let us have faith that right makes might, and in that faith let us to the end dare to do our duty as we understand it.

> –Abraham Lincoln, speech at Cooper Union (February 27, 1860).

Ne scutica dignum horribili sectere flagello.

Don't pursue with a horrible scourge what only deserves a switch.

−Horace, *Sat.* 1.3.119.

Let the punishment fit the crime.

−Popular saying.

Knowledge

🏛 **Nec scire fas est omnia.**

Nor is it proper to know all things.
> –Horace, *Carm.* 4.4.22.

That's a little too much information.
> –Popular saying.

🏛 **Sine doctrina vita est quasi mortis imago.**

Without learning, life is sort of simulation of death.
> –Cato, *Dist.* 3.1.

A learned man is an idler who kills time with study.
> –George Bernard Shaw, "Maxims for Revolutionists," *Man and Superman* (1903).

🏛 **Vivere est cogitare.**

To live is to think.
> –Cicero, *Tusc.* 5.111.

τὸ γὰρ αὐτὸ νοεῖν ἐστίν τε καὶ εἶναι.

For thinking and being are the same thing.
> –Parmenides, frag. 3 (D-K).

Cogito, ergo sum. (I think therefore I am.)
> –René Descartes, *Principles of Philosophy* (1644). He writes this elsewhere, but in French.

Latin

 Non tam praeclarum est scire Latine quam turpe nescire.

It is not so remarkable to know Latin as it is shameful not to know it.

–Cicero, *Brut.* 140.

I have not the advantage of a classical education and no man should, in my judgment, accept a degree he cannot read.

–Millard Fillmore, on turning down an honorary degree from Oxford in 1855 because it was written in Latin.

Law & Order

🏛 ἃ [γράμματα] μηδὲν τῶν ἀραχνίων
διαφέρειν, ἀλλ' ὡς ἐκεῖνα τοὺς
μὲν ἀσθενεῖς καὶ λεπτοὺς τῶν
ἁλισκομένων καθέξειν, ὑπὸ δὲ
τῶν δυνατῶν καὶ πλουσίων
διαρραγήσεσθαι.

*Laws differ not at all from spider webs. They hold fast the
weak and fragile whom they seize, but are torn apart by the
powerful and the rich.*

–Plutarch, *Sol.* 5.2.

One of the Seven was wont to say that laws
were like cobwebs; where the small flies were
caught, and the great brake through.

–Francis Bacon, *Apothegms*, no. 181
(1625).

🏛 τῆς δὲ κακῆς τε καὶ αἰσχρᾶς παιδείας
ἐν πόλει ἆρα μή τι μεῖζον ἕξεις
λαβεῖν τεκμήριον ἢ τὸ δεῖσθαι
ἰατρῶν καὶ δικαστῶν ἄκρων.

*You will find no surer sign of bad and shameful education
in a city than the need for outstanding doctors and jury
members.*

–Plato, *Resp.* 405a.

ὥσπερ ὅπου φάρμακα πολλὰ καὶ ἰατροὶ
πολλοί, ἐνταῦθα νόσοι πλεῖσται, οὕτω
δὴ καὶ ὅπου νόμοι πλεῖστοι, ἐκεῖ καὶ
ἀδικίαν εἶναι μεγίστην.

*Just as wherever there are many drugs and doctors there
are many diseases, so too is it that wherever there are the
most laws there is the greatest injustice.*

–Arcesilaus, quoted in Stobaeus 4.1.92.

Corruptissima re publica, plurimae leges.

*When the republic was the most corrupt, there were the
most laws.*

–Tacitus, *Ann.* 3.27.

When there are too many policemen, there can
be no individual liberty, when there are too
many lawyers, there can be no justice, and
when there are too many soldiers, there can
be no peace.

–Lin Yutang, *Between Tears and Laughter,*
ch. 8 (1943).

Aequo animo poenam, qui meruere, ferunt.

Those who have earned punishment bear it with equanimity.

–Ovid, *Am.* 2.7.12.

Sua quisque exempla debet aequo animo pati.

*Each person ought to endure with equanimity the precedents
he has set.*

–Phaedrus 1.26.12.

If you can't do the time, don't do the crime.
–Popular saying.

🏛 **Si quotiens peccant homines sua fulmina mittat / Iuppiter, exiguo tempore inermis erit.**

If Juppiter were to send forth his lightning bolts every time people sin, he would soon be out of ammunition.
–Ovid, *Tr.* 2.33–34.

If he [God] is just, why fear that he will punish the creatures that he has filled with weaknesses?
–Percy Bysshe Shelley, *The Necessity of Atheism* (1811), widely attributed online, but the phrase is not found in the text.

🏛 **Bonis nocet quisquis pepercerit malis.**

He harms good folk who forgives the bad.
–Pseudo-Seneca, *Mor.* 114; also in some collections of Publilius Syrus.

Spare the rod and spoil the child.
–Popular saying.

🏛 **Cavendum est etiam, ne maior poena, quam culpa sit.**

We must take care that the punishment is not in excess of the crime.
–Cicero, *Off.* 1.89.

Noxiae poena par esto.

Let the penalty be equal to the injury.

> –Cicero, *Leg.* 3.11.

Let the punishment fit the crime.

> –Popular saying.

 ## Delicta maiorum immeritus lues.

Though guiltless you will pay for the transgressions of your ancestors.

> –Horace, *Carm.* 3.6.1.

Culpam maiorum posteri luunt.

Descendants pay for their ancestors' sins.

> –Quintus Curtius 7.5.35.

The sins of the father / are to be laid upon the children.

> –William Shakespeare, *The Merchant of Venice*, act 3 scene 5 (1596–97).

 ## In hominem dicendum est igitur, quum oratio argumentationem non habet.

Since, then, his speech contains no proof, we must attack the individual.

> –Cicero, *Flac.* 23.

Get even with people. If they screw you, screw them back ten times as hard. I really believe it.

> –Donald Trump, speech before National Achievers Congress (2011).

Learning

🏛 **Discipulus est prioris posterior dies.**
The following day is the pupil of the previous one.
 –Publilius Syrus 146.

The difference between ancients and moderns
is that the ancients asked what have we
experienced, and moderns asked what can we
experience.
 –Alfred North Whitehead, *Adventures in
Ideas*, ch. 15 (1933).

🏛 **Dediscit animus sero quod didicit diu.**
The mind is slow to unlearn what it learned early on.
 –Seneca, *Tro.* 633.

As the twig is bent, so grows the tree.
 –Popular saying arising from Alexander
Pope, "Essay on Man: Epistle I," *Moral
Essays* (1733–34): "'Tis education
forms the common mind; / just as the
twig is bent, the tree's inclined."

Old habits die hard.
 –Popular saying.

🏛 οὐ γὰρ παίζουσι μανθάνοντες· μετὰ
λύπης γὰρ ἡ μάθησις.
People learning are not at play; for learning comes with pain.
 –Aristotle, *Pol.* 1339a.

Nosse volunt omnes, mercedem solvere nemo.

Everyone wants to know, but no one wants to pay the price.

–Juvenal 7.157.

No pain, no gain

–Popular saying.

🏛 ## Emendatio pars studiorum longe utilissima.

Correction is by far the most useful part of study.

–Quintilian 10.4.1.

The only kind of writing is rewriting.

–Ernest Hemingway, *A Moveable Feast*
(1964), attributed but apparently
incorrectly.

🏛 ## Non pudeat, quae nescieris, te velle doceri. Scire aliquid laus est; culpa est, nil discere velle.

Do not be ashamed that you want to learn things you do not know. To know something is praiseworthy; not wanting to learn is the fault.

–Cato, *Dist.* 4.29.

Nec me pudet fateri nescire quod nesciam.

Nor does it embarrass me to admit that I don't know what I don't know.

–Cicero, *Tusc.* 1.60.

Learn to say "I don't know." If used when
appropriate, it will be often.

–Donald Rumsfeld, *Rumsfeld's Rules*
(2013).

Life's Ups & Downs

🏛 Cito enim arescit lacrima, praesertim in alienis malis.

A tear dries quickly, especially when it is for the woes of others.
—Cicero, *Part.* 17.57; cf. *Inv. rhet.* 1.56.

I never knew any man in my life who could not bear another's misfortunes perfectly like a Christian.

—Alexander Pope, *Thoughts on Various Subjects*, 77 (1727).

By trying we can easily learn to endure adversity. Another man's I mean.

—Mark Twain, *Following the Equator*, epigraph to ch. 39 (1897).

🏛 Quivis beatus, versa rota fortunae, ante vesperum potest esse miserrimus.

Anyone who is sublimely happy can, through a turn of the wheel of fortune, be totally miserable before evening.
—Ammianus Marcellinus 26.8.13.

ὡς ἡμέρα κλίνει τε κἀνάγει πάλιν ἅπαντα τἀνθρώπεια.

How a day first lays low and then raises up all things human!
—Sophocles, *Aj.* 131.

Let the world, then, take notice, when Fortune
has the will to ruin a man, how many divers
[*sic*] ways she takes!
> –Benvenuto Cellini, *Autobiography*, ch.
> 113; translation, John Addington
> Symonds (1558–66).

🏛 Urbes constituit aetas, hora dissolvit. Momento fit cinis, diu silva.

*An age established cities. An hour destroyed them. A long
standing forest becomes ash in the blink of an eye.*
> –Seneca, *Q Nat.* 3.27.2.

What goes up, must come down; spinning wheel
got to go round.
> –David Clayton-Thomas (of rock band
> Blood, Sweat & Tears), "Spinning
> Wheel," song (1968).

🏛 Tolluntur in altum / ut lapsu graviore ruant.

People are raised on high so that they can rush to a graver fall.
> –Claudian, *In Ruf.* 1.22–23. Claudian is
> speaking of the unjust.

Excelsis multo facilius casus nocet.

Misfortune much more easily harms those on high.
> –Publilius Syrus 189.

Saepius ventis agitatur ingens pinus.

*More often than not it is the tall pine that is shaken by the
wind.*
> –Horace, *Carm.* 2.10.9.

The bigger they are, the harder they fall.
–Popular saying.

The trouble ain't that there is too many fools, but
that the lightning ain't distributed right.
–Mark Twain, quoted in Merle Johnson,
ed., *More Maxims of Mark* (1927).

🏛 Multa ceciderunt ut altius surgerent.

Many things have fallen so that they can rise up even higher.
–Seneca, *EM* 91.13.

Saepe Iovis telo quercus adusta viret.

Often an oak, charred by Jupiter's thunderbolt, flourishes.
–Ovid, *Tr.* 4.9.14.

What we've learned over this year is that hope is
making a comeback. It is making a comeback.
–Michelle Obama, campaign rally
(February 18, 2008).

It's not whether you get knocked down, it's
whether you get up.
–Vince Lombardi, attributed.

🏛 Melius in malis sapimus, secunda rectum auferunt.

*We grow wiser in bad times; prosperous times snatch rectitude
away.*
–Seneca, *EM* 94.74.

Adversity is sometimes hard upon a man; but for one man who can stand prosperity, there are a hundred that will stand adversity.

> –Thomas Carlyle, "The Hero as a Man of Letters," *On Heroes, Hero-Worship, and the Heroic in History* (1840). Apparently this is the source for a quote misattributed to Abraham Lincoln, "Nearly all men can stand adversity, but if you want to test a man's character, give him power."

🏛 Miscentur tristia laetis.

Sad times are mixed in with happy ones.

> –Ovid, *Fast.* 6.463.

You've got to take the bitter with the sweet.

> –Popular saying.

🏛 Non possunt primi esse omnes omni in tempore.

Everyone can't be first all the time.

> –Decimus Laberius, quoted in Macrobius, *Sat.* 2.7.9.

You can't win them all.

> –Popular saying.

The most important thing in the Olympic Games is not to win but to take part. The important thing in this life is not the victor but the contest.

> –Baron Pierre de Coubertin, founder of the modern Olympics, attributed, perhaps falsely.

Nihil enim semper floret.

For nothing is in bloom all the time.

–Cicero, *Phil.* 11.39.

Nothing lasts forever.

–Popular saying.

 ## Malum malo aptissimum.

Evil is most suited to evil.

–Livy 1.46. In other words, evil attracts
similar evil.

It's one damn thing after another.

–Popular saying.

It never rains but it pours.

–Popular saying.

 ## Ignis aurum probat, miseria fortes viros.

Fire tests gold, misfortune brave men.

–Seneca, *Prov.* 5.10.

He knows not his own strength that hath not
met adversity.

–Ben Jonson, attributed in James Boswell,
Life of Samuel Johnson (1780).

Love & Hate

Love

Totus vero iste, qui vulgo appellatur amor—nec hercule invenio quo nomine alio possit appellari—tantae levitatis est, ut nihil videam quod putem conferendum.

Really, that thing which is commonly called love—and by Hercules I can't find any other name by which to call it—is of such exceeding triviality that I see nothing that I think can be compared to it.

–Cicero, *Tusc.* 4.68.

We love without reason, and without reason we hate.

–Jean-François Regnard, *Les folies amoureuses* (1704).

Omnia vincit amor; et nos cedamus amori.

Love conquers all; let us, too, yield to love.

–Vergil, *Ecl.* 10.69.

"All You Need Is Love"

–John Lennon and Paul McCartney (of rock band the Beatles), title of song (1967).

Nemo in amore videt.

No one in love sees.

–Propertius 2.14.18.

Love is blind.

–Popular saying.

 # Ut ameris, amabilis esto.

In order to be loved, be lovable.

–Ovid, *Ars* 2.107.

Si vis amari, ama.

If you wish to be loved, love!

–Seneca, *EM* 9.6.

If you would be loved, love, and be lovable.

–Benjamin Franklin, attributed, falsely
but ubiquitously on the internet.

 # Amans iratus multa mentitur sibi.

An angry lover lies to himself a lot.

–Publilius Syrus 13.

Human beings have a demonstrated talent
for self-deception when their emotions are
stirred.

–Carl Sagan, *Cosmos* (1980).

When one is in love one begins by deceiving
one's self. And one ends by deceiving others.
That is what the world calls a romance.

–Oscar Wilde, *A Woman of No
Importance*, act 3 (1893).

🏛 Amantium irae, amoris integratio'st.

Lovers' quarrels are the renewal of love.

–Terence, *An.* 555.

A lovers' spat, he said. You know how it is. Boy
meets girl, girl wants boy dead. An everyday
story, really.

–David Gemmell, *Quest for Lost Heroes*
(1990).

🏛 In venere semper certat dolor et gaudium.

In love, sorrow and joy always contend with each other.

–Publilius Syrus 306.

You think you're gonna break up, then she says
she wants to make up.

–Eric Stewart and Graham Gouldman (of
rock band 10cc), "The Things We Do
for Love," song (1976).

🏛 Litore quot conchae, tot sunt in amore dolores.

There are as many woes in love as there are shells on the beach.

–Ovid, *Ars* 2.519.

There are as many forms of love as there are
moments in time.

–Attributed to Jane Austen widely on
the internet; in fact, from the script
of Patricia Rozema's film adaptation
of *Mansfield Park* (1999).

Difficilest longum subito deponere amorem.

It is hard suddenly to lay aside a long-time love.
–Catullus 76.13.

Love is so short, forgetting is so long.
–Pablo Neruda, "Tonight I Can Write" (1924).

 ## Semper in absentes felicior aestus amantes. Elevat assiduous copia longa viros.

The heat of love is always more fruitful toward absent lovers. A ready supply diminishes the appeal of persistent lovers.
–Propertius 2.33c.43.

Absence makes the heart grow fonder.
–Popular saying.

Familiarity breeds contempt.
–Popular saying.

Hate

 ## Marcet sine adversario virtus.

Without an adversary strength wastes away.
–Seneca, *Prov.* 2.3.

He that wrestles with us strengthens our nerves, and sharpens our skill. Our antagonist is our helper.
–Edmund Burke, *Reflections on the Revolution in France* (1790).

🏛 ## Proverbium iactatur "Totidem hostes esse quot servos." Non habemus illos hostes, sed facimus.

"So many slaves, so many enemies," says the proverb. They are not enemies when we get them. We make them so.

−Seneca, *EM* 47.5.

No one is born hating another person because of the color of his skin, or his background, or his religion. People must learn to hate, and if they can learn to hate, they can be taught to love, for love comes more naturally to the human heart than its opposite.

−Nelson Mandela, *Long Walk to Freedom* (1994).

Luck

 ἢ δοκοῦσί τί σοι τυφλῶν διαφέρειν
ὁδὸν ὀρθῶς πορευομένων οἱ ἄνευ
νοῦ ἀληθές τι δοξάζοντες;

*Or does it seem to you that those who hold opinions without
knowedge are any different from blind men who happen to
take the right road?*

–Plato, *Resp.* 506c.

Even a blind squirrel finds an acorn now and
then.

–Popular saying.

 θέλω τύχης σταλαγμὸν, ἢ φρενῶν
πίθον.

I'd rather a drop of luck than a pithos of wits.

–Menander, *Mon.* 240. A *pithos* was a
large clay storage pot.

I'd rather be lucky than good.

–Vernon Louis "Lefty" Gomez, Yankees
pitcher, winner of five World Series.

 **Fortunam citius reperias quam
retineas.**

*You can find good fortune more quickly than you can hold
onto it.*

–Publilius Syrus 198.

Fortuna vitrea est; tum cum splendet, frangitur.

Fortune is made of glass; it breaks when it is resplendent.
–Publilius Syrus 219.

Fortuna nimium quem fovet stultum facit.

Whom Fortune favors too much, she makes a fool.
–Publilius Syrus 203.

Fortuna plus homini quam consilium valet.

Luck does more for a person than planning.
–Publilius Syrus 222.

The harder I practice, the luckier I get.
–Gary Player, quoted in Guy Yocom,
"Gary Player: Take It from the Man in
Black," *Golf Digest* (October 2002).

Luck is the residue of design.
–Branch Rickey, attributed.

Marriage

 οὐ μὲν γάρ τι γυναικὸς ἀνὴρ ληΐζετ᾽
ἄμεινον / τῆς ἀγαθῆς, τῆς δ᾽ αὖτε
κακῆς οὐ ῥίγιον ἄλλο.

*A man wins no better prize than a good wife and nothing
colder than a bad one.*

–Hesiod, *Op.* 702–3.

Keep your eyes wide open before marriage,
half shut afterwards.

–Benjamin Franklin, *Poor Richard's
Almanack* (1766).

 δεῖ δὲ μὴ τοῖς ὄμμασι γαμεῖν.

No one should marry using just his eyes.

–Plutarch, *Coniug.* 141c.

Marry in haste, repent at leisure.

–Popular saying; cf. William
Shakespeare, *The Taming of the
Shrew*, act 3 scene 2 (1590–91):
"Who woo'd in haste, and means
to wed at leisure."

 τοὺς μὲν νέους μηδέπω, τοὺς δὲ
πρεσβυτέρους μηδεπώποτε

Young men, not yet, and old men never at all

–Diogenes of Sinope, quoted in
Diogenes Laertius 6.2.54, on the
proper time for a man to get
married.

Writing is like getting married. One should never commit oneself until one is amazed at one's luck.

–Iris Murdoch, *The Black Prince* (1973).

Quid enim iucundius quam uxori tam carum esse, ut propter hoc tibi carior fias?

What is more delightful than to be so dear to your wife that this very fact makes you dearer to yourself?

–Seneca, *EM* 104.5.

νομίζω δὲ γυναῖκα κοινωνὸν ἀγαθὴν οἴκου οὖσαν πάνυ ἀντίρροπον εἶναι τῷ ἀνδρὶ ἐπὶ τὸ ἀγαθόν.

In my opinion, a wife who is a good partner running the house is entirely of equal weight to the man toward its good.

–Xenophon, *Oec.* 3.15.

There is no more lovely, friendly, and charming relationship, communion, or company than a good marriage.

–Martin Luther, *Table Talk* (1569).

Mind & Body

Stress

🏛 τὸ σήμερον μέλει μοι, τὸ δ' αὔριον τίς οἶδεν;

My concern is today. As for tomorrow, who knows?

> −Anacreontea 8.9 (Loeb, Greek Lyric II).

πῖνε παῖζε· θνητὸς βίος, ὀλίγος οὐπὶ γῆ χρόνος· ἀθάνατος ὁ θάνατός ἐστιν, ἂν ἅπαξ τις ἀποθάνῃ.

Drink! Play! Life is mortal, brief is our time on the earth; death is deathless once someone has actually died.

> −Amphis, *Gynaecocratia* (frag. 8, CAF / frag. 1, FCG).

Eat, drink, and be merry, for tomorrow we die.

> −Popular saying; cf. Eccles. 8:15 and Luke 12:19.

🏛 τὰ τόξα οἱ ἐκτημένοι, ἐπεὰν μὲν δέωνται χρᾶσθαι, ἐντανύουσι· εἰ γὰρ δὴ τὸν πάντα χρόνον ἐντεταμένα εἴη, ἐκραγείη ἄν.

People with bows string them only when they need to use them; for if they were strung all the time, they would break.

> −Herodotus 2.173.

Cito rumpes arcum, semper si tensum habueris, / at si laxaris, cum voles, erit utilis.

You will quickly break a bow if you always keep it strung. But if you unstring it, it will be of use when you want it.

–Phaedrus 3.14.10.

Continua messe senescit ager.

A field grows old from constant harvesting.

–Ovid, *Ars* 3.82.

All work and no play makes Jack a dull boy.

–Popular saying.

🏛 Ignis, quo clarior fulsit, citius exstinguitur.

The brighter a fire burns, the sooner it goes out.

–Seneca, *Cons. Marc.* 23.4.

Your candle burned out long before your legend ever did.

–Elton John and Bernie Taupin, "Candle in the Wind," song (1973, about Marilyn Monroe; 1997, changed slightly for Princess Diana).

My candle burns at both ends; it will not last the night; / but, ah, my foes, and oh, my friends—/ it gives a lovely light.

–Edna St. Vincent Millay, "First Fig," *A Few Figs from Thistles* (1922).

🏛 ## Olim mensis Decembris mensis erat, nunc annus.

Once upon a time December was a month—now it's a year.

> –Seneca, *EM* 18.1, quoting an anonymous author who is complaining that the feast of Saturnalia has become a year-long thing, taking away from a quiet, contemplative life.

Only ____ more shopping days until Christmas

> –On signs everywhere, appearing earlier and earlier each year.

Exercise

🏛 ## κακῶν γὰρ ὄντων μυρίων καθ' Ἑλλάδα / οὐδὲν κάκιόν ἐστιν ἀθλητῶν γένους.

Of the thousands of evils besetting Greece, none is worse than the race of athletes.

> –Euripides, *Autolycus* frag. 282.

In America, it is sport that is the opiate of the masses.

> –Russell Baker, *New York Times* (October 3, 1967).

Serious sport has nothing to do with fair play. It is bound up with hatred, jealousy, boastfulness, disregard of all rules and sadistic pleasure in witnessing violence: in other words it is war minus the shooting.

> –George Orwell, "The Sporting Spirit," *Tribune* (December 14, 1945).

🏛 Stulta est enim, mi Lucili, et minime conveniens litterato viro, occupatio exercendi lacertos et dilatandi cervicem ac latera firmandi.

This business of exercising one's muscles, widening one's neck and shaping up one's sides is a foolish business, my dear Lucilius, and far from suitable for an educated man.
—Seneca, *EM* 15.2.

Exercise is bunk. If you are healthy, you don't need it: if you are sick you shouldn't take it.
—Henry Ford, attributed.

🏛 Hodiernus dies solidus est; nemo ex illo quicquam mihi eripuit. Totus inter stratum lectionemque divisus est. Minimum exercitationi corporis datum, et hoc nomine ago gratias senectuti. Non magno mihi constat; cum me movi, lassus sum. Hic autem est exercitationis etiam fortissimis finis.

Today has been unbroken. No one snatched any of it away from me. It was entirely divided between rest and reading. A little bit was given over to bodily exercise, and I give thanks for this in the name of old age. This is because it costs me little. When I move, I'm tired. This, after all, is the goal of exercise for even the fittest.
—Seneca, *EM* 83.3.

I have never taken any exercise, except sleeping
and resting, and I never intend to take any.
Exercise is loathsome. And it cannot be any
benefit when you are tired; and I was always
tired.

> –Mark Twain, speech at Delmonico's in
> New York City on the occasion of his
> seventieth birthday (1905).

Misdeeds

🏛 **Prosperum ac felix scelus / virtus vocatur.**

A successful and profitable crime is called virtue.
                              –Seneca, *Herc. F.* 251–52.

Quae fuerant vitia, mores sunt.

What used to be vices are customs.
                              –Seneca, *EM* 39.6.

A crime preserved in a thousand centuries ceases to be a crime, and becomes a virtue. This is the law of custom, and custom supersedes all other forms of law.
                              –Mark Twain, *Following the Equator*, ch. 63 (1897).

🏛 **ἀδικεῖ πολλάκις ὁ μὴ ποιῶν τι, οὐ μόνον ὁ ποιῶν τι.**

Very often someone doing nothing commits injustice, not just someone doing something.
                              –Marcus Aurelius 9.2.5.

Nam tua res agitur; paries cum proximus ardet / et neglecta solent incendia sumere vires.

Because it is your business when your neighbor's house is on fire. Neglected fires have a habit of picking up strength.
                              –Horace, *Epist.* 1.18.84–85.

All that is necessary for evil to prosper is that good men do nothing.

> –Edmund Burke, attributed. Found in myriad variants, but no original source is definite.

🏛 ## Male parta, male dilabuntur.

Things born badly will fall badly to ruin.

> –Cicero, *Phil.* 2.65.

But, Clifford, tell me, didst thou never hear / that things ill-got had ever bad success?

> –William Shakespeare, *Henry VI, Part 3,* act 2 scene 2 (1591).

🏛 ## τὰ ἐλάχιστα ληπτέον τῶν κακῶν.

One must choose the least of the evils.

> –Aristotle, *Eth. Nic.* 1109a.

The lesser of two evils

> –Popular saying.

🏛 ## Neque enim est quisquam tam malus, ut videri velit.

For no one is so bad that he wants to appear that way.

> –Quintilian 3.8.45.

There's a good spot tucked away somewhere in everybody. You'll be a long time finding it sometimes.

> –Mark Twain, "Refuge of the Derelicts," unpublished manuscript (1905–6).

🏛 ## Maiores [dicebant] . . . malum quidem nullum esse sine aliquo bono.

Our ancestors used to say that there is nothing bad without some good in it.

–Pliny the Elder 27.9.

Every cloud has its silver lining.

–Popular saying.

Money (See also Seven Deadly Sins—Greed)

🏛 **Pecunia una regimen est rerum omnium.**

Money alone is what controls everything.
—Publilius Syrus 506.

Money makes the world go around.
—Fred Ebb, "Money, Money," song in
Cabaret (1966).

🏛 **Semper pauper eris, si pauper es, Aemiliane; / dantur opes nullis nunc nisi divitibus.**

If you're poor, Aemilianus, you always will be poor. Nowadays riches are given to none but the rich.
—Martial, *Epig.* 5.81.1.

The rich get richer and the poor get poorer.
—Popular saying; cf. "There's nothing
sure; the rich get rich and the poor get
poor," Richard A. Whiting, Raymond
B. Egan, Gus Kahn, "Ain't We Got
Fun," song (1921).

🏛 **Simplici cura constant necessaria; in delicias laboratur.**

Necessities require mere attention; luxuries require labor.
—Seneca, *EM* 90.16.

He does not possess wealth; it possesses him.
—Benjamin Franklin, *Poor Richard's
Almanack* (1734).

🏛 **Esto, ut nunc multi, dives tibi, pauper amicis.**

Be, as so many are today, a rich man to yourself, a pauper to your friends.

–Juvenal 5.113.

Charity begins at home.

–Popular saying.

🏛 **Nullum [studium] suspicio, nullum in bonis numero, quod ad aes exit.**

I defend no line of study and number none among the good, whose aim is making money.

–Seneca, *EM* 88.1, defending the liberal arts.

I insist that the object of all true education is not to make men carpenters, it is to make carpenters men.

–W. E. B. DuBois, *The Negro Problem*, ch. 2 (1903).

🏛 **Ne dubita, cum magna petis, impendere parva.**

When you seek a lot, do not hesitate to spend a little.

–Cato, *Dist.* 1.35.

Penny wise and pound foolish

–Popular saying.

🏛 **Pauperis est numerare pecus.**

Counting one's flock is the sign of a poor man.

–Ovid, *Met.* 13.824.

If you have to ask the price, you can't afford it.
> –J. P. Morgan, attributed; supposed
> answer to someone asking how much
> his yacht cost.

🏛 **Emas non quod opus est, sed quod necesse est. Quod non opus est, asse carum est.**

You should not buy what is needed, but what is necessary. What isn't needed is too expensive at even a penny.
> –Cato the Elder, quoted in Seneca, *EM*
> 94.27.

Most of the luxuries, and many of the so-called comforts of life, are not only not indispensable, but positive hindrances to the elevation of mankind.
> –Henry David Thoreau, "Economy,"
> *Walden* (1854).

🏛 **Ad vivendum velut ad natandum is melior qui onere liberior.**

For living as for swimming, the one with the least baggage is the one better off.
> –Apuleius, *Apol.* 21.5.

Less is more.
> –Robert Browning, "Andrea del Sarto,"
> *Men and Women* (1855).

Necessity

🏛 οὐ γὰρ ἔστι διδάσκαλος οὐδεὶς τούτων κρείττων τῆς ἀνάγκης.

There is no greater teacher of these things than necessity.
> –Xenophon, *Cyr.* 2.2.13.

Fac de necessitate virtutem.

Make a virtue out of necessity.
> –St. Jerome, *Ep.* 54.6.

Necessity is the mother of invention.
> –Popular saying; not from Plato, *Resp.*
> 369c, as is often asserted.

🏛 **Qui e nuce nucleum esse vult, frangit nucem.**

A person who wants the meat of a nut, breaks the nut.
> –Plautus, *Curc.* 55.

If you want to make an omelet, you have to break some eggs.
> –Popular saying.

🏛 **Necessitas ultimum et maximum telum est.**

Necessity is the last, and the greatest, weapon.
> –Livy 4.28.5, slightly modified.

Thanne is it wysdom, as thynketh me, / to maken vertu of necessité.
> –Geoffrey Chaucer, "Knight's Tale,"
> *Canterbury Tales* (1387–1400).

Namque inscitiast / advorsum stimulum calces.

Because it is insanity for you to kick back against the goad.
–Terence, *Phorm.* 76–77.

I said, "Who am I to blow against the wind?"
–Paul Simon, "I Know What I Know,"
song (1986).

You've got to go with the flow.
–Popular saying.

Old Age

🏛 Singula de nobis anni praedantur euntes; / eripuere iocos, Venerem, convivia, ludum.

The passing years despoil us of things, one by one. They have snatched away jokes, Venus, dinner parties, play.

–Horace, *Epist.* 2.55.

Years steal / fire from the mind, as vigor from the limb; / and life's enchanted cup but sparkles near the brim.

–Lord Byron (George Gordon), *Childe Harold's Pilgrimage* 3.8 (1816).

🏛 πολιὰ χρόνου μήνυσις, οὐ φρονησέως.

Gray hairs are a sign of time, not of wisdom.

–Menander, *Mon.* 705.

An old goat is never the more reverend for his beard.

–Thomas Fuller, *Gnomologia*, no. 646 (1732).

Wrinkles should merely indicate where the smiles have been.

–Mark Twain, widely attributed, probably falsely.

ἡ γελωμένη πολιὰ καὶ ῥυτὶς ἐμπειρίας
μάρτυς ἐπιφαίνεται.

*Gray hair and wrinkles that are made fun of are really
witnesses of experience.*

–Plutarch, *An seni.* 789d.

Si albicapillus hic, videtur, neutiquam ab ingenio senex.

*Even though he has white hair, he is by no means old in
spirit.*

–Plautus, *Mil.* 631.

Age does not bring you wisdom, age brings you
wrinkles.

–Estelle Getty, star of the television show
Golden Girls, quoted in her *New York
Times* obituary (July 23, 2008).

There may be snow on the roof, but there is a fire
in the furnace.

–Popular saying.

 Non sum ego qui fueram. Quid
inanem proteris umbram?

*I am not who I once was. Why do you tread on an empty
shadow?*

–Ovid, *Tr.* 3.11.25.

Nemo nostrum idem est in senectute qui fuit iuvenis.

None of us is the same in old age as he was in youth.

–Seneca, *EM* 58.22.

I ain't what I used to be, but who the hell is?
> –Dizzy Dean, attributed.

Yesterday; I'm not half the man I used to be.
> –John Lennon and Paul McCartney (of
> rock band the Beatles), "Yesterday,"
> song (1965).

🏛 τοὺς πρεσβυτέρους τιμᾶν [δεῖ].

One should respect one's elders.
> –Pythagoras, quoted in Diogenes
> Laertius 8.1.22.

Respect your elders.
> –Popular saying.

🏛 οὔ τοι σύμφορόν ἐστι γυνὴ νέα ἀνδρὶ
γέροντι

Let me tell you, a young woman is not suitable for an old man.
> –Theognis, frag. 457.

Look, I'd go out with women my own age, but
there are no women my age.
> –Spoken by George Burns at ninety-two
> in *18 Again!*, film (1988). Screenplay
> by Josh Goldstein and Jonathan
> Prince.

🏛 **Nemo enim est tam senex qui se
annum non putet posse vivere.**

No one is so old that he doesn't think he can live one more year.
> –Cicero, *Sen.* 24.

How can I die? I'm booked.

> –George Burns, quoted in his *New York Times* obituary (March 10, 1996). Burns had arranged to perform on his one-hundredth birthday at the London Palladium Theatre. He died on March 9 of that same year.

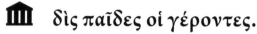 δὶς παῖδες οἱ γέροντες.

The old are children a second time.

> –Aristophanes, *Nub.* 1417.

πάλιν γὰρ αὖθις παῖς ὁ γηράσκων ἀνήρ.

A man growing old is a child once more.

> –Sophocles, *Peleus* frag. 487.

When all my days are ending / and I have no song to sing, / I think that I shall not be too old / to stare at everything; / as I stared once at a nursery door / or a tall tree and a swing.

> –G. K. Chesterton, "Second Childhood" (1922).

τὸ γῆρας ἔλεγεν ὅρμον εἶναι τῶν κακῶν.

He used to say that old age is the harbor for bad things.

> –Bion, quoted in Diogenes Laertius 4.7.48.

Old age is a shipwreck.

> –Charles de Gaulle, attributed.

On Women

🏛 καίτοι τί διαφέρει γυναῖκας ἄρχειν ἢ τοὺς ἄρχοντας ὑπὸ τῶν γυναικῶν ἄρχεσθαι;

Now what difference does it make whether the women rule or the rulers are ruled by the women?

> –Aristotle, *Pol.* 1269b.

Si sine uxore pati possemus ... omnes ea molestia careremus; sed quoniam ita natura tradidit, ut nec cum illis satis commode, nec sine illis ullo modo vivi possit, saluti perpetuae potius quam brevi voluptati consulendum est.

If we could endure existence without wives, we would all be rid of that nuisance. But, since nature has decreed that in no way can we either live very comfortably with them or without them, we should consider our long-term welfare rather than our short-term pleasure.

> –Aulus Gellius 1.6.2, quoting from a speech given by Metellus Numidicus, in which he encouraged citizens to get married.

Women, can't live with them, can't live without them.

> –Popular saying, often attributed to Erasmus, probably incorrectly.

Varium et mutabile semper femina.

Woman is an ever changing and mutable thing.

–Vergil, *Aen.* 4.569.

Aut amat aut odit mulier: nihil est tertium.

A woman either loves or hates: there is no third option.

–Publilius Syrus 6.

It's a woman's prerogative to change her mind.

–Popular saying.

 οἱ μὲν ἄνδρες γεγόνασί μοι γυναῖκες, αἱ δὲ γυναῖκες ἄνδρες.

My men have become women and my women men.

–Herodotus 8.88, spoken by the Persian king Xerxes as he watched the Battle of Salamis in 480 BCE. Ships commanded by his men were having no success against the Greeks, but the female commander, Queen Artemisia of Caria, was notable for her success and bravery.

Dux femina facti.

The leader of the deed is a woman.

–Vergil, *Aen.* 1.364, describing Dido's incredible accomplishment of founding Carthage as a refugee.

Ginger Rogers did everything Fred Astaire did, except backwards and in high heels.

–Often attributed to Ginger Rogers herself, Governor Ann Richards, and, especially, Faith Whittlesey, ambassador to Switzerland during

the Reagan administration. Some
point to the syndicated cartoon
Frank and Ernest, in which a woman
addresses two men, all standing next
to a sign advertising a Fred Astaire
film festival. Turning to the men,
she says, "Sure he was great, but
don't forget that Ginger Rogers did
everything *he* did . . . backwards and
in high heels" (May 3, 1982).

🏛 ὡς τρὶς ἂν παρ' ἀσπίδα / στῆναι
θέλοιμ' ἂν μᾶλλον ἢ τεκεῖν ἅπαξ.
*I would rather stand in battle with a shield three times than
give birth once.*

–Euripides, *Med.* 250–51.

ἡ μὲν γὰρ ὠδίνουσα καὶ δυσφοροῦσα
πρὸς τοὺς κατακλίνοντας αὐτὴν ἔλεγε,
"πῶς δ' ἂν ἡ κλίνη ταῦτα θεραπεύσειεν
οἷς ἐπὶ τῆς κλίνης περιέπεσον;"
*A woman enduring a difficult labor kept saying to those who
were trying to make her go to bed, "How can a bed cure
what I contracted on a bed?"*

–Plutarch, *Coniug.* 143e. A similar story
occurs in Phaedrus 1.18.

Having a baby is like trying to push a grand
piano through a transom.

–Alice Roosevelt Longworth, attributed.

Opinion

🏛 ἡμῶν δ’ ὅσα καὶ τὰ σώματ’ ἐστὶ τὸν
ἀριθμὸν / καθ’ ἑνός, τοσούτους ἔστι
καὶ τρόπους ἰδεῖν.

*As many bodies as there are of us, there are, one for one, that
many ways of thinking.*

–Philemon, frag. 89 (CAF) / frag. 93 (K-A).

Quot homines tot sententiae.

There are as many opinions as there are people.

–Terence, Phorm. 454.

There are as many opinions as there are experts.

–Franklin D. Roosevelt, radio address
(June 12, 1942).

🏛 οὐκ ᾔσθησαι τὰς ἄνευ ἐπιστήμης
δόξας, ὡς πᾶσαι αἰσχραί;

*Have you never noticed that opinions without knowledge are all
disgraceful?*

–Plato, Resp. 506c.

The opinions that are held with passion are
always those for which no good ground
exists; indeed the passion is the measure
of the holder's lack of rational conviction.
Opinions in politics and religion are almost
always held passionately.

–Bertrand Russell, "Introduction: On the
Value of Scepticism," Sceptical Essays
(1961).

Opportunity

🏛 Rem tibi quam nosces aptam dimittere noli; fronte capillata, post est Occasio calva.

Don't lose a thing that you know is good for you. Opportunity has hair in front but is bald in back.

—Cato, *Dist.* 2.26.

When Fortune comes, seize her in front with a sure hand, because behind she is bald.

—Leonardo da Vinci, *Notebooks* (ca. 1500).

🏛 Dum loquimur fugerit invida aetas: carpe diem, quam minimum credula postero.

Even as we speak, envious time will have flown past. Seize the day and trust in tomorrow as little as you can.

—Horace, *Carm.* 1.11.7–8.

Accipe quam primum; brevis est occasio lucri.

Take it as soon as you can; the opportunity for profit is short.

—Martial, *Epig.* 8.9.3.

Make hay while the sun shines.

—Popular saying.

Strike while the iron is hot.

—Popular saying.

Occasio aegre offertur, facile amittitur.

Opportunity is offered reluctantly, lost easily.
> –Publilius Syrus 496.

Opportunity doesn't knock twice.
> –Popular saying.

 ## Deliberando saepe perit occasio.

An opportunity is often lost by thinking it over.
> –Publilius Syrus 163.

He who hesitates is lost.
> –Popular saying.

Optimism & Pessimism

🏛 μὴ φῦναι τὸν ἄπαντα νικᾷ λόγον.

Not to be born wins out over every other idea.
–Sophocles, OC 1224–25.

> The best of all things is something entirely outside your grasp: not to be born, not to be, to be nothing. But the second-best thing for you—is to die soon.
>
> –Friedrich Nietzsche, *The Birth of Tragedy*, ch. 3 (1872).

🏛 **Utique secunda expecto, malis paratus sum.**

Anyway, I look for good times and am prepared for bad times.
–Seneca, EM 88.17.

> The optimist proclaims that we live in the best of all possible worlds; and the pessimist fears this is true.
>
> –James Branch Cabell, *The Silver Stallion: A Comedy of Redemption* (1926).

🏛 **Nulla tam bona est fortuna de qua nihil possis queri.**

There is no fortune so good that you can find nothing to complain about in it.
–Publilius Syrus 429.

If you expect the worst from a person, you can't ever be disappointed.

> –Anthony Burgess, *The Wanting Seed* (1962).

🏛 Omnis habet sua dona dies.

Every day has its gifts.

> –Martial, *Epig.* 8.78.7.

"Always Look on the Bright Side of Life"

> –Eric Idle, title of song in *Monty Python's Life of Brian* (1976).

🏛 Ut quisque est vir optimus, ita difficillime esse alios improbos suspicatur.

The better a man is, the more difficulty he has suspecting that others are dishonest.

> –Cicero, *Q. fr.* 1.12.

I never met a man I didn't like.

> –Will Rogers, "Rogers Gets Six Shiny Dimes from Oil King," nationally syndicated column, no. 219 (1927).

Patience

 Adhuc tua messis in herba est.

Your harvest is still on the plant.
                    –Ovid, *Her.* 17.263.

Don't count your chickens before they're
hatched.
                    –Popular saying.

 Cuivis dolori remedium est patientia.

The cure for any woe is patience.
                    –Publilius Syrus 111.

Gutta cavat lapidem, consumitur anulus usu.

Water drops hollow out a stone; a ring is worn down by use.
                    –Ovid, *Pont.* 4.10.5.

Caducis / percussu crebro saxa cavantur.

Stones are hollowed out by being frequently struck by water drops.
                    –Ovid, *Pont.* 2.7.39–40.

Slow and steady wins the race.
                    –Popular saying, traceable back to
                    Aesop's "The Hare and the Tortoise."

Much rain wears the marble.
                    –William Shakespeare, *Henry VI Part 3*,
                    act 3 scene 3 (1591).

Nihil non acerbum prius quam maturum fuit.

Nothing is ripe that wasn't sour before.

–Publilius Syrus 441.

Every sweet hath its sour, every evil its good.

–Ralph Waldo Emerson,
"Compensation," *Essays* (1841).

 Optimum est pati quod emendare non possis.

The best thing is to endure what you cannot change.

–Seneca, *EM* 107.9.

What can't be cured must be endured.

–Popular saying.

Perseverance

 Apelli fuit alioqui perpetua consuetudo numquam tam occupatam diem agendi, ut non lineam ducendo exerceret artem quod ab eo in proverbium venit.

Further, it was Apelles's invariable custom never to pass so busy a day that he didn't have time for the exercise of his art by at least drawing a line. And from this it passed over into a proverb.

–Pliny the Elder 35.84. The proverb was "Nulla dies sine linea" (No day without a line), which is the motto of the Art Students League of New York on West Fifty-Seventh Street in New York City.

Post malam segetem serendum est.

After a bad harvest one must sow again.
–Seneca, *EM* 81.1.

If at first you don't succeed, try, try again.
–Popular saying.

Pettiness

 Parvum parva decent.
Small things befit a small person.

–Horace, *Epist.* 1.7.44.

Little things affect little minds.

–Benjamin Disraeli, *Sibyl, or The Two Nations* (1845).

Philosophy

 Nihil tam absurde dici potest quod non dicatur ab aliquo philosophorum.

There is nothing that can be so absurdly said that has not been said by but some philosopher or other.

−Cicero, *Div.* 2.119.

Postremo nemo aegrotus quicquam somniat tam infandum, quod non aliquis dicat philosophus.

To sum it up, no sick person has ever dreamed up anything so absurd that some philosopher or another might say it.

−Varro, frag. of a Menippean satire named *Eumenides,* preserved in Nonius (Lindsay and Onions 1.79).

A philosopher is a blind man in a dark room looking for a black cat that isn't there. A theologian is the man who finds it.

−H. L. Mencken, attributed.

Philosophy, n. A route of many roads leading from nowhere to nothing.

−Ambrose Bierce, *The Devil's Dictionary* (1911).

Plans

🏛 ## Homo semper aliud, Fortuna aliud cogitat.

Man always plans one thing, Fortune another.
> –Publilius Syrus 253.

Everyone has a plan until they get punched in the mouth.
> –Mike Tyson, quoted by Mike Berardino in *The South Florida Sun Sentinel* (November 9, 2012).

🏛 ## Sperat quidem animus: quo eveniat, dis in manu est.

Indeed, the spirit has hopes, but how it may turn out is in the hands of the gods.
> –Plautus, *Bacch.* 144.

Man plans and God laughs.
> –Yiddish proverb.

If you want to make God laugh, tell him about your plans.
> –Woody Allen, attributed.

🏛 ## Miserum est opus, igitur, demum fodere puteum, ubi sitis fauces tenet.

It's a sad business, then, finally to dig a well when thirst has you by the throat.
> –Plautus, *Mostell.* 380.

When the well's dry they know the worth of
water.

-Benjamin Franklin, *Poor Richard's
Almanack* (1746).

 ## Numquam desunt consulta duobus.

Where two take counsel there is never a lack of plans.

-Silius Italicus 15.351.

Two heads are better than one.

-Popular saying.

Politics & Power

οὐ μὲν γάρ τι κακὸν βασιλευέμεν.
For it's no bad thing to be king.
> –Homer, *Od.* 1.392.

It's good to be the king.
> –Spoken by Mel Brooks playing Louis
> XVI in *History of the World Part I*, film
> (1981). Screenplay by Mel Brooks.

ὁ ἄνθρωπος φύσει πολιτικὸν ζῷον.
Man is by nature a political animal.
> –Aristotle, *Pol.* 1278b The adjective
> *politikon* really means "of the polis,"
> that is, the city-state, and was applied
> to various animals, like bees and ants,
> that live in orderly societies.

Humiles laborant, ubi potentes dissident.
The humble struggle when the powerful quarrel.
> –Phaedrus 1.30.1.

When the elephants fight, the grass gets
trampled.
> –African proverb.

μόνοι γὰρ τόν τε μηδὲν τῶνδε
μετέχοντα οὐκ ἀπράγμονα, ἀλλ᾽
ἀχρεῖον νομίζομεν.
We [Athenians] alone consider one not participating in these
[political] affairs not as being uninvolved, but as useless.
> –Thucydides 2.40.2.

Politics should be the part-time profession of every citizen.

–Dwight D. Eisenhower, address recorded for the Republican Lincoln Day dinners (January 28, 1954).

🏛 οἴκοι μὲν λέοντες, / ἐν μάχῃ δ᾽ ἀλώπεκες

Lions at home, but foxes in battle

–Aristophanes, *Pax* 1189–90.

Domi leones, foris vulpes

Lions at home, foxes abroad

–Petronius 44.

I am sometimes a fox and sometimes a lion. The whole secret of government lies in knowing when to be the one or the other.

–Napoleon Bonaparte, attributed.

🏛 ἔνθα γὰρ σοφίης δέει, βίης ἔργον οὐδέν.

Where wisdom is required, there is no need for force.

–Herodotus 3.127.

Victory attained by violence is tantamount to defeat, for it is momentary.

–Mahatma Gandhi, *Satyagraha Leaflet No. 13* (May 3, 1919).

κινδυνεύει πόλις ἀνδρῶν ἀγαθῶν εἰ
γένοιτο, περιμάχητον ἂν εἶναι τὸ μὴ
ἄρχειν ὥσπερ νυνὶ τὸ ἄρχειν.

*If a city of good men should happen to exist, there would
probably be as great a struggle not to govern as there is now
to do so.*

—Plato, *Resp.* 347d.

It could probably be shown by facts and figures
that there is no distinctly native American
criminal class except Congress.

—Mark Twain, *Following the Equator,*
epigraph to ch. 8 (1897).

 τούτων δὲ τῶν ἀγγέλων ἐστὶ οὐδὲν ὅ
τι θᾶσσον παραγίνεται θνητὸν
ἐόν . . . τοὺς οὔτε νιφετός, οὐκ
ὄμβρος, οὐ καῦμα, οὐ νὺξ ἔργει μὴ
οὐ κατανύσαι τὸν προκείμενον αὐτῷ
δρόμον.

*Nothing mortal is faster than these messengers. Neither snow
nor rain, heat nor night keeps them from accomplishing
their appointed route.*

—Herodotus 8.98.

Neither snow nor rain nor heat nor gloom of
night stays these couriers from the swift
completion of their appointed rounds.

—Words carved above the entrance to the
James A. Farley Post Office in New
York City and often thought to be the
motto of the USPS. In fact, the USPS
has no official motto.

🏛 Auferre, trucidare, rapere, falsis nominibus imperium; atque, ubi solitudinem faciunt, pacem appellant.

To ravage, to slaughter, to seize—this they misname as "empire." And where they make a desert, they call it peace.

–Calgacus, quoted in Tacitus, *Agr.* 30.5.

Scorched earth policy

–Common description of the military policy of destroying anything that might be useful to the enemy.

🏛 Vis consili expers mole ruit sua.

Power devoid of deliberation crashes under its own weight.

–Horace, *Carm.* 3.4.65.

A man may build himself a throne of bayonets, but he cannot sit on it.

–Boris Yeltsin, televised speech (October 4, 1993).

🏛 εἰ τιν' ἂν δοκεῖς / ἄρχειν ἑλέσθαι ξὺν φόβοισι μᾶλλον ἢ / ἄτρεστον εὕδοντ';

Or do you think that anyone chooses to rule amid fears rather than to sleep untroubled?

–Sophocles, *OT* 584–86.

Dictators ride to and fro upon tigers which they dare not dismount. And the tigers are getting hungry.

–Winston Churchill, "Armistice—or Peace?," *Evening Standard* (November 11, 1937).

🏛 Nulla aconita bibuntur fictilibus.

Poisons aren't drunk out of clay cups.

–Juvenal 10.25.

Venenum in auro bibitur.

Poison is drunk from a golden cup.

–Seneca, *Thy.* 453.

Necesse est multos timeat quem multi timent.

One whom many fear must fear many.

–Decimus Laberius, frag. 3 (Ribbeck 2.253), quoted in Seneca, *Ira* 2.11.3.

Uneasy lies the head that wears a crown.

–William Shakespeare, *Henry IV Part 2*, act 3 scene 1 (1596–97).

🏛 Ars prima regni est posse in invidia pati.

A king's first skill is to be able to endure ill will.

–Seneca, *Herc. F.* 353.

Regnare non vult, esse qui invisus timet.

One who fears being hated does not want to rule.

–Seneca, *Phoen.* 654.

You've got to grow a thick skin.
                    –Popular saying.

🏛 ἄρχε, πρῶτον μαθὼν ἄρχεσθαι,
ἄρχεσθαι γὰρ μαθὼν ἄρχειν
ἐπιστήσῃ.

Rule, having learned to be ruled, for having learned to be ruled,
you will know how to rule.
                    –Solon, quoted in Diogenes Laertius
                    1.2.60.

Nemo autem regere potest, nisi qui et regi.

However, no one can rule unless he can also be ruled.
                    –Seneca, *Ira* 2.15.4.

How shall I be able to rule over others, that have
not full power and command of myself?
                    –François Rabelais, *Gargantua and*
                    Pantagruel, ch. 1.52 (1532–64).

🏛 **Iucundiorem autem faciet libertatem**
servitutis recordatio.

The memory of servitude will make freedom more pleasant.
                    –Cicero, *Phil.* 3.36.

Men would rather be starving and free than fed
in bonds.
                    –Pearl S. Buck, *What America Means to*
                    Me (1943).

Quis custodiet ipsos / custodes?

Who will guard the guards themselves?

> –Juvenal 6.347–48 (= Loeb 6.O31–32).
> Juvenal speaks of incidents in which
> supposed eunuchs who served as
> chaperones for women nevertheless
> misbehaved.

Lisa: If you're the police, who will police the police?

Homer: I don't know. Coast Guard?

> –*The Simpsons*, "Homer the Vigilante,"
> season 5, episode 11 (aired January 6,
> 1994). Written by John Swartzwelder.

Lycus: I had a bad experience with an officer to whom I had sold a virgin.

Pseudolus: What happened?

Lycus: She turned out to be a dud.

Pseudolus: A dud virgin? How could that happen?

Lycus: You see, the fellow who sold me the dud virgin also sold me a dud eunuch.

> –Bert Shevelove and Larry Gelbart, *A
> Funny Thing Happened on the Way to
> the Forum* (1962).

🏛 ## Sic cum inferiore vivas, quemadmodum tecum superiorem velis vivere.

You should treat an inferior the way you would like to be treated by your superior.

—Seneca, *EM* 47.11.

Be nice to people on the way up because you'll meet them on the way down.

—Wilson Mizner, attributed by Stuart B. McIver, *Dreamers, Schemers and Scalawags* (1994).

🏛 ## ἰσχυρὸν ὄχλος ἐστίν, οὐκ ἔχει δὲ νοῦν.

A mob is a strong thing, but it has no mind.

—Menander, *Mon.* 265.

The nose of a mob is its imagination. By this, at any time, it can be quietly led.

—Edgar Allan Poe, "Marginalia," *Southern Literary Messenger*, vol. 15 (1849).

Procrastination

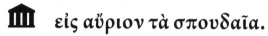 εἰς αὔριον τὰ σπουδαῖα.

Serious matters tomorrow!

> –Archias of Thebes, quoted in Plutarch,
> *Pel.* 10.4.

Nothing with gods, nothing with fate; weighty affairs will just have to wait!

> –Stephen Sondheim, "Comedy Tonight,"
> song in *A Funny Thing Happened on the
> Way to the Forum* (1962).

Differ! Habent parvae commoda magna morae.

Put it off! Small delays have great advantages.

> –Ovid, *Fast.* 3.394.

Do not put off until tomorrow what can be put off till day-after-tomorrow just as well.

> –Mark Twain, attributed in Merle
> Johnson, ed., *More Maxims of Mark*
> (1927).

Dimidium facti qui coepit habet.

One who has begun has half the deed done.

> –Horace, *Epist.* 1.2.40.

ἀρχὴ δέ τοι ἥμισυ παντός. Incipe!
Dimidium facti est, coepisse: supersit
dimidium; rursum hoc incipe, et
efficies.

*The beginning is half of everything. Start! To begin is half
the deed. Let half remain. Begin it again and you will get
it done.*

> –Ausonius, *Epig.* 15. The Greek that
> Ausonius begins with is also found
> in Lucian, *Somn.* 3 and *Herm.* 3; cf.
> Hesiod, *Op.* 40.

Well begun is half done.

> –Popular saying.

🏛 Tolle moras: semper nocuit deferre paratis.

*Away with delays! Putting things off has always harmed the
prepared.*

> –Lucan 1.281.

He who hesitates is lost.

> –Popular saying.

Prudence

 Id facere laus est quod decet, non
quod licet.

There is praise in doing what one should, not what is allowed.
—Seneca, *Oct.* 454.

Hitler was undoubtedly a genius but he lacked
self-control. He recognized no limits.
Otherwise the thousand-year Reich would
have lasted more than twelve years.

—Wilhelm Frick (March 10, 1946),
reported in Leon Goldensohn and R.
Gellately, *The Nuremberg Interviews*
(2004).

Plus scire satius est quam loqui.

It is preferable to know more than you say.
—Plautus, *Epid.* 60.

εἰδὼς σίγα.

Keep quiet, even if you know.
—Solon, *Apothegms of the Seven Sages*, frag.
2.10a (D-K).

A shut mouth catches no flies.
—English proverb.

A still tongue makes a wise head.
—English proverb.

ἄκουε πολλὰ, λάλει καίρια.

Listen a lot, speak when it's time.

> –Bias of Priene, originally quoted in
> Demetrius of Phaleron and preserved
> in Stobaeus 3.1.172 (= frag. 114,
> Wehrli); more accessible in Laks,
> 2.145 no. 11.

Remember not only to say the right thing in
the right place, but far more difficult still, to
leave unsaid the wrong thing at the tempting
moment.

> –Benjamin Franklin, attributed.

 ἡ γὰρ σιωπὴ τοῖς σοφοῖσιν ἀπόκρισις.

In the eyes of the wise, silence is an answer.

> –Euripides, frag. 977, preserved in
> Plutarch, *Vit. pud.* 532f; attributed by
> some to Menander, *Mon.* 307 (= *FCG*
> 222).

ἔστι καὶ σιγὰς ἀκίνδυνον γέρας.

Silence too is a danger-free reward.

> –Simonides, frag. 582.

Est et fideli tuta silentio / merces.

There is safe profit in loyal silence.

> –Horace, *Carm.* 3.2.25–26.

Tacent: satis laudant.

They are silent. They are praising it well enough.

> –Terence, *Eun.* 476.

His silence is more eloquent than words.

> –Thomas Carlyle, "The Hero as Poet," *On Heroes, Hero-Worship, and the Heroic* (1840).

🏛 ## Exigua est virtus praestare silentia rebus. / At contra gravis est culpa tacenda loqui.

It's a small virtue to keep silent about things. On the other hand, it is a grave fault to speak about things about which one should keep silent.

> –Ovid, *Ars* 2.603–4.

Virtutem primam esse puto, compescere linguam: / proximus ille deo est qui scit ratione tacere.

I think the highest virtue is to control one's tongue; that one is nearest to a god who knows when it is reasonable to be silent.

> –Cato, *Dist.* 1.3.

Three may keep a Secret, if two of them are dead.

> –Benjamin Franklin, *Poor Richard's Almanack* (1735).

🏛 ## Scelera impetu, bona consilia mora valescunt.

Crimes grow strong from rushing, good planning from delay.

> –Tacitus, *Hist.* 1.32.

Haste makes waste.

> –Popular saying.

🏛 νῆ᾽ ὀλίγην αἰνεῖν, μεγάλῃ δ᾽ ἐνὶ φορτία
θέσθαι.

Praise a small boat, but put your cargo onto a big one.
                    −Hesiod, *Op.* 643.

Love your neighbor: yet don't pull down your
hedge.
                    −Benjamin Franklin, *Poor Richard's
                    Almanack* (1754).

🏛 **In ipsa securitate animus ad difficilia
se praeparet.**

*It is in the very midst of security that your spirit should prepare
itself for hard times.*
                    −Seneca, *EM* 18.6.

οἱ τοῦ λύχνου χρείαν ἔχοντες ἔλαιον
ἐπιχέουσιν.

Those who have need of a lamp put oil in it.
                    −Anaxagoras, quoted in Plutarch, *Per.*
                    16.7.

The time to repair the roof is when the sun is
shining.
                    −John. F. Kennedy, second State of the
                    Union address (Jan 11, 1962).

Put something away for a rainy day.
                    −Popular saying.

Relativity

 Est ipsa cupiditati tarda celeritas.

Even speed itself is slow to one who is eager.

–Publilius Syrus 134, in some collections.

O vita misero longa, felici brevis!

O how long is life for a miserable man and how short for a happy one!

–Publilius Syrus 485.

When a man sits with a pretty girl for an hour, it seems like a minute. But let him sit on a hot stove for a minute and it's longer than any hour. That's relativity.

–Albert Einstein, said to his secretary, Helen Dukas, to pass on to reporters and non-specialists.

 Non omnia eadem aeque omnibus, ere, suavia esse scito.

Master, keep in mind that the same things are not equally agreeable to all people.

–Plautus, *Asin.* 641.

I refuse to accept other people's ideas of happiness for me. As if there's a "one size fits all" standard for happiness.

–Kanye West, *Thank You and You're Welcome* (2009).

Religion

🏛 αἰεὶ τε Διὸς κρείσσων νόος ἠέ περ
ἀνδρῶν.

Zeus's mind always is greater than that of men.

–Homer, *Il.* 16.688.

Dis aliter visum.

It seemed otherwise to the gods.

–Vergil, *Aen.* 2.428.

Man proposes, God disposes.

–Popular saying, with its origin in
Thomas à Kempis, *The Imitation of
Christ*, book 1.19 (ca. 1418): "Homo
proponit, sed Deus disponit" (Man
proposes, but God disposes).

🏛 **Di nos quasi pilas homines habent.**

The gods treat us like balls in a game.

–Plautus, *Capt.* 22.

As flies to wanton boys are we to th' gods; / they kill us for their sport.

–William Shakespeare, *King Lear*, act 4
scene 1 (1605–6).

🏛 **Saepius illa religio peperit scelerosa
atque impia facta.**

*That very religion has rather frequently given birth to criminal
and impious deeds.*

–Lucretius 1.83–84.

In the so-called ages of faith, when men really did believe the Christian religion in all its completeness, there was the Inquisition, with all its tortures; there were millions of unfortunate women burned as witches; and there was every kind of cruelty practiced upon all sorts of people in the name of religion.

–Bertrand Russell, *Why I Am Not a Christian* (1927).

Reputation

🏛 **Multo deformius amittere quam non adsequi laudem.**

It is much more shameful to lose praise than never to acquire it.
–Pliny the Younger, *Ep.* 8.24.9

Character is much easier kept than recovered.
–Thomas Paine, *The American Crisis* (1819).

🏛 **Suum cuique decus posteritas rependit.**

Posterity pays each man his appropriate reward.
–Tacitus, *Ann.* 4.35.

Time will tell.
–Popular saying.

Revenge

 Inimicum ulcisci vitam accipere est alteram.

To get revenge on an enemy is to receive another life.
–Publilius Syrus 270.

Revenge is sweet.
–Popular saying.

Rules to Live By

🏛 εὔκολον ἔφασκε τὴν εἰς ᾅδου ὁδόν.

He used to say that the road to Hades is easy.

–Bion, quoted in Diogenes Laertius
4.7.49.

Facilis descensus Averno.

Easy is the descent to Avernus [the Underworld].
–Vergil, *Aen.* 6. 126.

That's the start of a slippery slope.
–Popular saying.

The road to hell is paved with good intentions.
–Popular saying.

🏛 **Non ut diu vivamus curandum est,
sed satis.**

Care shouldn't be taken to live long, but satisfactorily.
–Seneca, *EM* 93.2.

Only those are fit to live who do not fear to die.
–Theodore Roosevelt, *The Great
Adventure* (1918).

🏛 νεανίσκου πολλὰ λαλοῦντος ἔφη,
"τὰ ὦτά σου εἰς τὴν γλῶτταν
συνερρύηκεν."

*When a young lad was chattering away, he said, "Your ears
have flowed into your tongue."*

–Zeno, quoted in Diogenes Laertius,
7.1.21.

"διὰ τοῦτο," εἶπε, "δύο ὦτα ἔχομεν, στόμα
δὲ ἕν, ἵνα πλείω μὲν ἀκούωμεν ἥττονα
δὲ λέγωμεν."

*"This is why," he said, "we have two ears but one mouth—so
that we can hear more but speak less."*

–Zeno, quoted in Diogenes Laertius 7.1.23.

φιλήκοον εἶναι μᾶλλον ἢ φιλόλαλον.

Being a good listener is better than being a good talker.

–Cleobulus, quoted in Diogenes Laertius
1.6.92.

I always tell kids, you have two eyes and one
mouth. Keep two open and one closed. You
never learn anything if you're the one talking.

–Gordie Howe, NHL great, quoted in Jeff
Jacobs, "My Friend, Gordie Howe,"
Hartford Courant (June 10, 2016).

When people talk, listen completely. Most
people never listen.

–Ernest Hemingway, letter of advice to a
young writer, reported in *Life* (January
10, 1949).

🏛 **Quod vult habet qui velle quod satis
est potest.**

He has what he wants who can want what is enough.

–Publilius Syrus 626.

You can't always get what you want, but if you
try sometime, you find you get what you need.

–Mick Jagger and Keith Richards (of rock
band the Rolling Stones), "You Can't
Always Get What You Want," song (1969).

Same & Different

🏛 εἰ γάρ τις προθείη πᾶσι ἀνθρώποισι
ἐκλέξασθαι κελεύων νόμους
τοὺς καλλίστους ἐκ τῶν πάντων
νόμων, διασκεψάμενοι ἂν ἑλοίατο
ἕκαστοι τοὺς ἑωυτῶν.

*If someone should make a proposal to all peoples, ordering
them to choose the best of all customs, then each, after
careful examination, would choose its own.*
> –Herodotus 3.38.

We must respect the other fellow's religion, but
only in the sense and to the extent that we
respect his theory that his wife is beautiful
and his children smart.
> –H. L. Mencken, *Minority Report: H. L.*
> *Mencken's Notebooks* (1956).

🏛 ## Tam similem quam lacte lacti est

As identical as milk is to milk
> –Plautus, *Mil.* 240, describing twin
> women.

Neque lact' lactis magis est simile, quam ille ego similest mihi.

Milk is no more like milk than I am to me.
> –Plautus, *Amph.* 601. The slave Sosia is
> staring at Mercury, who is costumed
> to be an exact copy of him.

Videsne ut in proverbio sit ovorum inter se similitudo?

Don't you see that, as the proverb goes, one egg is like another?

–Cicero, *Acad.* 2.57.

Like two peas in a pod

–Popular saying.

Scholarship & Pedantry

🏛 πολυμαθίη νόον οὐ διδάσκει.

Wide learning does not teach understanding.

> –Heraclitus, quoted in Diogenes Laertius
> 9.1.1.

Faciuntne intelligendo ut nil intelligent?

*By knowing so much, don't they see to it that they know
nothing?*

> –Terence, *An.* prologue 17.

Erudition, n. Dust shaken out of a book into an
empty skull.

> –Ambrose Bierce, *The Devil's Dictionary*
> (1911).

A scholar is a man with this inconvenience, that
when you ask him his opinion of any matter,
he must go home and look up his manuscripts
to know.

> –Ralph Waldo Emerson, *Journals* (June
> 1855).

All shuffle there; all cough in ink; / all wear the
carpet with their shoes; / all think what other
people think.

> –William Butler Yeats, "The Scholars"
> (1917).

Scire tuum nihil nisi te scire hoc sciat alter?

Is your knowledge nothing unless someone else knows that you know it?

–Persius 1.27.

Pedantry is the dotage of knowledge.

–Holbrook Jackson, *Anatomy of Bibliomania* (1930).

Seven Deadly Sins

Note: The sins are not listed alphabetically, but according to a mnemonic learned long ago on many a Sunday morning amid dreams of donuts to come—beware PALE GAS.

Pride

🏛 **Adhuc neminem cognovi poetam qui sibi non optimus videretur.**

So far I have met no poet who doesn't seem the best—to himself.

–Cicero, *Tusc.* 5.63.

Intellexit . . . gallum in suo sterquilino plurimum posse.

He understood that a cock is most powerful on its own dunghill.

–Seneca, *Apoc.* 7.

Cock of the walk

–Popular saying.

🏛 **Non tu scis, quom ex alto puteo sursum ad summum escenderis, / maximum periculum inde esse, a summo ne rursum cadas?**

Don't you know that when you have climbed up out of a deep well, that's when the danger is greatest of falling back in from the top?

–Plautus, *Mil.* 1150–51.

The bigger they are, the harder they fall.
–Popular saying.

The higher the monkey climb, the more he expose.
–Spoken by Whoopi Goldberg playing Clara Mayfield in *Clara's Heart*, film (1988); from a common Jamaican saying. Screenplay by Mark Medoff.

Avarice

 ᾧ ὀλίγον οὐχ ἱκανόν, ἀλλὰ τούτῳ γε οὐδὲν ἱκανόν.
Nothing's enough for one to whom a little is not enough.
–Epicurus, quoted in Aelian, *VH* 4.13.

Non qui parum habet, sed qui plus cupit, pauper est.
It's not the one who has too little, but the one who desires more who is poor.
–Seneca, *EM* 2.6.

Divitiae meae sunt; tu divitiarum es.
My wealth belongs to me; you belong to your wealth.
–Seneca, *Vit.* 22.5.

Wealth is not his that has it, but his that enjoys it.
–Benjamin Franklin, *Poor Richard's Almanack* (1736).

Multa petentibus desunt multa.
For those seeking much, much is lacking.
–Horace, *Carm.* 3.16.42–43.

Non opibus mentes hominum curaeque levantur.

People's minds and cares are not lightened by wealth.

—Tibullus 3.21.

Inopiae desunt multa, avaritiae omnia.

Poverty lacks much, avarice everything.

—Publilius Syrus 275.

Few rich men own their property. The property owns them.

—Robert Ingersoll, speech to the
McKinley League in New York City
(October 29, 1896).

🏛 Cum classicum cecinit, [pauper] scit non se peti.

When the war trumpet sounds, the poor man knows they're not after him.

—Seneca, *EM* 17.3. Seneca is touting one
of the advantages of a simple life—no
one goes to war to acquire a hut.

Avaritia vero senilis quid sibi velit, non intellego. Potest enim quicquam esse absurdius quam, quo viae minus restet, eo plus viatici quaerere?

*I don't understand what avarice in old age hopes to achieve.
Can anything be more absurd than, when less of the
journey remains, to seek out more baggage?*

—Cicero, *Sen.* 66.

It is better to live rich than to die rich.

> –Samuel Johnson, quoted in James
> Boswell, *Life of Samuel Johnson*, entry
> for April 17, 1778 (1791).

Crescentem sequitur cura pecuniam.

Care follows money as it grows.

> –Horace, *Carm.* 3.16.19.

Crescit amor nummi quantum ipsa pecunia crescit.

The love of money grows at the same pace as the money.

> –Juvenal 14.139.

If we command our wealth, we shall be rich and free; if our wealth commands us, we are poor indeed.

> –Edmund Burke, *Letters on a Regicide
> Peace* (1796).

Minus habeo quam speravi: sed fortasse plus speravi quam debui.

I have less than I hoped; but perhaps I hoped for more than I deserved.

> –Seneca, *Ira* 3.30.3.

The Earth provides enough to satisfy every man's need but not for every man's greed.

> –Mahatma Gandhi, quoted in Pyarelal
> Nayyar, *Mahatma Gandhi: The Last
> Phase*, vol. 10 (1958).

🏛 ## Nihil tam munitum quod non expugnari pecunia possit.

Nothing is so strongly fortified that it can't be taken with money.

–Cicero, *Verr.* 1.4.

He refuseth the bribe but putteth forth his hand.

–English proverb.

Lust

🏛 ## Ἀφροδίτα μὲν οὐκ ἔστι, μάργος δ᾽ Ἔρως οἷα <παῖς> παίσδει.

There is no Aphrodite, just wild Eros, playing like a child.

–Alcman, frag. 58.

Love is blind.

–Popular saying.

🏛 ## Ἔρος δ᾽ ἐτίναξέ μοι φρένας, ὡς ἄνεμος κὰτ ὄρος δρύσιν ἐμπέτων.

Love shook my heart like a wind rushing down a mountain onto oak trees.

–Sappho, frag. 47, quoted in Maximus of Tyre, *Orations* 18.9.

I think you got hit by the thunderbolt.

–Spoken by Angelo Infanti playing Fabrizio in *The Godfather,* film (1972). Screenplay by Francis Ford Coppola, Mario Puzo, and Robert Towne. Fabrizio, one of Michael Corleone's bodyguards in Sicily, says this after Corleone first sees Apollonia, soon to be his wife.

χρὴ τοιαύταις πλησιάζειν γυναιξὶν αἳ χάριν εἴσονται.

One should associate with the sorts of women who will be grateful.

> –Antisthenes, quoted in Diogenes Laertius 6.1.3. The verb πλησιάζειν implies sexual relations.

I repeat my former Advice, that in all your Amours you should prefer old Women to young ones. You call this a Paradox, and demand my Reasons. They are these: ... 8thly and Lastly They are so grateful!!

> –Benjamin Franklin, "Advice to a Young Man on the Choice of a Mistress" (June 25, 1745).

 Quidve tibi prodest viduas dormire puellas?

What profit is there to you [Io] that girls sleep alone?

> –Propertius 2.33a.17. Propertius laments that his love, Cynthia, has been worshipping the goddess Io ten nights running, and Io has thus deprived him of her company.

If a woman sleeps alone, it puts a shame on all men.

> –Spoken by Anthony Quinn playing Alexis Zorba in *Zorba the Greek*, film (1965). Screenplay by Michael Cacoyannis.

Envy

 ## Invidia, tanquam ignis, summa petit.

Envy, like fire, always seeks out the highest.

–Livy 8.31.

Tall poppy syndrome

–Australian phrase used to describe a national propensity to cut outstanding (and vainglorious) individuals down to size. The origin of this phrase lies in Herodotus 5.92, which tells the story of Periander, tyrant of Corinth, who sent a messenger to Thrasybulus, tyrant of Miletus, asking for advice on how to rule. Thrasybulus said nothing, but simply walked through a field of wheat with the man, lopping off all the tall stalks and discarding them. This was taken as advice for Periander to eliminate all his important challengers.

 ## παύροις γὰρ ἀνδρῶν ἐστι συγγενὲς τόδε, / φίλον τὸν εὐτυχοῦντ᾿ ἄνευ φθόνων σέβειν.

Few men have it in them to honor a friend who is doing well without envying him.

–Aeschylus, *Ag.* 832–33.

If you wish to be happy yourself, you must resign yourself to seeing others also happy.

–Betrand Russell, "The Science to Save Us from Science," *New York Times Magazine* (March 19, 1950).

Gluttony

 οἱ μὲν λοιποὶ ζῶσιν ἵν᾽ ἐσθίωσιν, αὐτος δε ἐσθίω ἵνα ζῶ.

The rest of people live to eat, but I eat to live.

> –Socrates, quoted in Stobaeus 17.22; cf.
> Diogenes Laertius 2.5.34.

Esse oportet ut vivas, non vivere ut edas.

You should eat in order to live, not live in order to eat.

> –Cicero, *Her.* 4.28.39.

Non ut edam vivo, sed ut vivam edo.

I do not live in order to eat; rather I eat in order to live.

> –Quintilian 9.3.85.

Eat to live, and not live to eat.

> –Benjamin Franklin, *Poor Richard's
> Almanack* (1733).

 ## Nemo liber est qui corpori servit.

No one is free who serves his body.

> –Seneca, *EM* 92.33.

What do you get when you guzzle down sweets?
Eating as much as an elephant eats? What are
you at getting terribly fat? What do you think
will come of that? I don't like the look of it.

> –Leslie Bricusse and Anthony Newley,
> "Oompa Loompa (Augustus)," song in
> *Willy Wonka & the Chocolate Factory*
> (1971).

Anger

🏛 **Ira quae tegitur nocet.**

It's hidden anger that does the harm.

—Seneca, *Med.* 153.

> I was angry with my friend: / I told my wrath,
> my wrath did end. / I was angry with my foe;
> / I told it not, my wrath did grow.
>
> —William Blake, "Christian Forbearance"
> (1794).

🏛 **Procellae, quanto plus habent virium, tanto minus temporis**

The stronger the storms, the shorter they last

—Seneca, *Q Nat.* 7.9.1

> Our passions are like convulsion fits, which
> make us stronger for the time, but leave us
> weaker forever after.
>
> —Variously attributed to Alexander Pope
> or Jonathan Swift.

🏛 **ἐν ὀργῇ μήτε τι λέγειν, μήτε πράσσειν [δεῖ].**

One should neither say nor do anything in anger.

—Pythagoras, quoted in Diogenes
Laertius 8.1.23.

Rei nulli prodest mora nisi iracundiae.

Delay helps nothing except anger.

—Publilius Syrus 628.

Maximum remedium irae mora est.

The best cure for anger is delay.

–Seneca, *Ira* 2.29.1.

ὅταν ὀργισθῇς, Καῖσαρ, μηδὲν εἴπῃς μηδὲ ποιήσῃς πρότερον ἢ τὰ εἴκοσι καὶ τέτταρα γράμματα διελθεῖν πρὸς ἑαυτόν.

Whenever you get angry, Caesar, you should not say or do anything until you go through the twenty-four letters of the alphabet to yourself.

–Plutarch, *Apoph. Rom.* 207c, quoting Athenodorus, Augustus's Stoic tutor.

When angry, count ten before you speak; if very angry a hundred.

–Thomas Jefferson, letter to Thomas Jefferson Smith (February 21, 1825).

When angry, count four. When very angry, swear.

–Mark Twain, *Pudd'nhead Wilson*, epigraph to ch. 10 (1894).

 ## Ira furor brevis est.

Anger is a short-lived madness.

–Horace, *Epist.* 1.2.62.

Anger is a wind which blows out the lamp of the mind.

–Robert Ingersoll, attributed.

Sloth

🏛 ἔργον δ᾽ οὐδὲν ὄνειδος. ἀεργίη δέ
τ᾽ ὄνειδος.

There is no shame in work. Idleness is the shame.
−Hesiod, *Op.* 311.

Vitanda est improba Siren—desidia.

The evil Siren of inactivity must be avoided.
−Horace, *Sat.* 2.3.14.

It takes application, a fine sense of value, and a
powerful community-spirit for a people to
have serious leisure, and this has not been the
genius of the Americans.
−Paul Goodman, *Growing Up Absurd*
(1960).

🏛 **Cernis ut ignavum corrumpant otia
corpus; / ut capiant vitium ni
moveantur aquae.**

*You see how leisure corrupts an idle body, how water becomes
stagnant unless it is moving.*
−Ovid, *Pont.* 1.5.5–6.

I like work: it fascinates me. I can sit and look at
it for hours. I love to keep it by me: the idea of
getting rid of it nearly breaks my heart.
−Jerome J. Jerome, *Three Men in a Boat*,
ch. 15 (1899).

Shame

 Epistula ... non erubescit.
A letter ... doesn't blush.

> –Cicero, *Fam.* 22.1, admitting to a friend
> that it is easier to ask for things by
> letter than face-to-face.

ἅπας ἐρυθριῶν χρηστὸς εἶναί μοι δοκεῖ.

*Everyone who can blush, it seems to me, must be a
worthwhile person.*

> –Menander, frag. 301 (Körte and
> Thierfelder).

Man is the only animal that blushes. Or needs to.

> –Mark Twain, *Following the Equator*,
> epigraph to ch. 27 (1897).

Sickness & Health

 ἄλλων ἰατρός, αὐτὸς ἕλκεσιν βρύων.

Doctor to others, he himself is bursting with sores.

> –Euripides, frag. 1086 from an unknown play.

Neque imitare malos medicos, qui in alienis morbis profitentur tenere se medicinae scientiam, ipsi se curare non possunt.

Do not imitate bad doctors, who claim they possess the art of healing other people's ills but are unable to cure themselves.

> –Cicero, *Fam.* 248.5. Servius Sulpicius, writing to Cicero and offering consolation for the death of Tullia, Cicero's daughter, telling him to follow his own philosophical advice.

Physician, heal thyself.

> –Popular saying, ultimately from Luke 4:23.

 οἱ ἰατροί, φησὶν ὁ Ἡράκλειτος, τέμνοντες, καίοντες, πάντῃ βασανίζοντες κακῶς τοὺς ἀρρωστοῦντας, ἐπαιτιῶνται μηδέν᾽ ἄξιον μισθὸν λαμβάνειν παρὰ τῶν ἀρρωστούντων.

Heraclitus says that doctors, cutting, burning, and foully torturing the sick in every way possible, demand an undeserved fee from them.

> –Quoted in Hippolytus, *Haer.* 9.10.3.

Though the doctors treated him, let his blood, and gave him medications to drink, he nevertheless recovered.

> –Leo Tolstoy, *War and Peace* (1869).

🏛 **Bona fama in tenebris proprium splendorem tenet.**

A good reputation has its own splendor, even in the dark/in dark times.

> –Publilius Syrus 83.

Old age and sickness bring out the essential character of a man.

> –Felix Frankfurter, quoted in Harlan Phillips, *Felix Frankfurter Reminisces* (1960).

🏛 **Perfer et obdura: dolor hic tibi proderit olim. / Saepe tulit lassis sucus amarus opem.**

Carry on and endure. This pain will be to your profit someday. A bitter potion has often brought relief to the weary.

> –Ovid, *Am.* 3.11a.8–9.

Ubi turpis est medicina, sanari piget.

When the medicine is vile, it is annoying to be healed.

> –Seneca, *Oed.* 517.

A bitter pill to swallow

> –Popular saying.

🏛 οὐκ ἔστι τὸ θεράπευμα τῆς ἀλγηδόνος ἄξιον.

The cure isn't worth the pain.

> –Plutarch, *Apoph. Rom.* 202b, citing the Roman general Marius, who had undergone an operation for varicose veins in one leg and refused to have the doctors work on the other.

The medicine is worse than the cure.

> –Popular saying.

🏛 ἐννοεῖν συνεχῶς πόσοι μὲν ἰατροὶ ἀποτεθνήκασι πολλάκις τὰς ὀφρῦς ὑπὲρ τῶν ἀρρώστων συσπάσαντες.

Always keep in mind how many physicians have died who so often furrowed their brows over the sick.

> –Marcus Aurelius 4.48.

Interviewer: Is it true that you smoke eight to ten cigars a day?

George Burns: That's true.

Int.: Is it true that you drink five martinis a day?

GB: That's true.

Int.: Is it true that you still surround yourself with beautiful young women?

GB: That's true.

Int.: What does your doctor say about all of this?

GB: My doctor is dead.

> –George Burns, reported variously in different interviews, a stock line in his later life.

Sympathy

 ἐκ τοῦ παθεῖν γίγνωσκε καὶ τὸ
συμπαθεῖν.

From being miserable, learn to commiserate as well.
  –Philemon, frag. 230 (*CAF*).

Oh, I have suffered / with those that I saw suffer.
  –William Shakespeare, *The Tempest*, act 1
  scene 2 (1610–11).

Taxes

🏛 **Praesidibus onerandas tributo provincias suadentibus rescripsit boni pastoris esse tondere pecus, non deglubere.**

To the governors who were encouraging him to oppress the provinces with taxes, he [Tiberius] wrote that it's the job of a good shepherd to shear the flock, not skin them.
—Suetonius, *Tib.* 32.2.

There is one difference between a tax collector and a taxidermist—the taxidermist leaves the hide.

–Mortimer Caplin, director of the IRS, quoted in *Time* (February 1, 1963).

🏛 **Neque enim quies gentium sine armis, neque arma sine stipendiis, neque stipendia sine tributis.**

Without arms, there is no rest among nations; no arms, without pay for the military; and no pay, without taxes.
–Tacitus, *Hist.* 4.74.

Taxes are the chief business of a conqueror of the world.

–George Bernard Shaw, *Caesar and Cleopatra*, act 2 (1901).

Teaching

 φύσεως καὶ ἀσκήσεως διδασκαλία δεῖται.

Teaching requires innate talent and training alike.
> –Protagoras, quoted in *Anecdota Graeca*
> (Cramer 1.171 / frag. 3, D-K).

Teachers are born, not made.
> –Popular saying.

 ὅλως τε σημεῖον τοῦ εἰδότος καὶ μὴ εἰδότος τὸ δύνασθαι διδάσκειν.

Generally speaking, the sign of knowing or of not knowing is the ability to teach.
> –Aristotle, *Metaph.* 981b.

A man who knows a subject thoroughly . . . can always teach it with success, no matter how little he knows of technical pedagogy.
> –H. L. Mencken, *Prejudices: Third Series*
> (1922).

 Idem et docenti et discenti debet esse propositum: ut ille prodesse velit, hic proficere.

A person teaching and a person learning should have the same end in view; that the latter wish to progress and the former to be of use.
> –Attalus, philosopher and Seneca's
> teacher, quoted in Seneca, *EM* 108.3.

Homines, dum docent, discunt.

When people teach, they learn.

–Seneca, *EM* 7.8.

Gaudeo discere, ut doceam.

I delight in learning, so that I might teach.

–Seneca, *EM* 6.4. These two sayings of Seneca are probably the ultimate source for the following otherwise unattested common Latin sayings: "Qui docet, discit" (He who teaches, learns); "Docendo disco" (I learn by teaching); "Doce ut discas" (Teach that you may learn).

Quod enim munus rei publicae offere maius, meliusve possumus quam si docemus, atque erudimus iuventutem.

For what greater or better gift can we offer the state than if we teach and educate our young?

–Cicero, *Div.* 2.4.

τῶν γονέων τοὺς παιδεύσαντας ἐντιμοτέρους εἶναι τῶν μόνον γεννησάντων· τοὺς μὲν γὰρ τὸ ζῆν, τοὺς δὲ τὸ καλῶς ζῆν παρασχέσθαι.

He used to say that those who educated children should be honored more than their parents, who merely gave birth to them. The one gave life, the other gave how to live well.

–Aristotle, quoted in Diogenes Laertius 5.1.19.

For the life of me I cannot fathom why we
expect so much from teachers and provide
them so little in return. . . . There was no
Plato without Socrates, and no John Coltrane
without Miles Davis.

> –Bill Moyers, "America 101," *Moyers on
> Democracy* (2008).

🏛 **Neque est omnino ars ulla, in qua
omnia quae illa arte effici possunt, a
doctore tradantur.**

*There is no art whatever in which all the things that can be
accomplished by that art are imparted by a teacher.*

> –Cicero, *De Orat.* 2.69.

If you teach a man anything he will never learn it.

> –George Bernard Shaw, *Back to
> Methuselah* (1922).

🏛 **Quanta autem dementia eius est,
quem clamores inperitorum
hilarem ex auditorio dimittunt?**

*How great is the madness of one whom the applause of the
inexperienced sends out of the lecture hall happy!*

> –Seneca, *EM* 52.11.

O popular applause! What heart of man / is
proof against thy sweet, seducing charms?

> –William Cowper, *The Task*, book 2, "The
> Progress of Error" (1785).

Temperance (See also Caution)

🏛 τὸ νικᾶν αὐτὸν αὐτὸν πασῶν νικῶν πρώτῃ τε καὶ ἀρίστη.

For one to conquer oneself is the first and best of all victories.
–Plato, *Leg.* 626e.

Nature, Mr. Allnutt, is what we are put in this world to rise above.

–Katharine Hepburn playing Rose Sayer in *The African Queen*, film (1951). Screenplay by James Agee and John Huston. Rose makes this response after Charlie Allnutt has overindulged in gin and explained, "It's only human nature."

🏛 **Video meliora proboque; / deteriora sequor.**

I see the better way and I approve of it, but I follow the worse.
–Ovid, *Met.* 7.20–21.

Abstainer, n. A weak person who yields to the temptation of denying himself a pleasure.

–Ambrose Bierce, *The Devil's Dictionary* (1911).

🏛 μηδὲν ἄγαν

Nothing too much

–Pausanias 10.24.1 and the *Suda* (= Loeb, *Elegiac Poetry*, 107). One of the aphorisms written on the temple wall at Delphi by the so-called Seven Wise Men and commonly attributed to Solon.

πάντων μὲν κόρος ἐστί.

All things have a point of satiety.

—Homer, *Il.* 13.636.

Nam id arbitror / apprime in vita esse utile ut ne quid nimis.

For I think this is especially useful for living one's life—that nothing be too much.

—Terence, *An.* 60–61.

Bonarum rerum consuetudo pessima est.

Getting accustomed to good times is quite a bad thing.

—Publilius Syrus 58.

As people do better, they start voting like Republicans . . . unless they have too much education and vote Democratic, which proves there can be too much of a good thing.

—Karl Rove, quoted in Nicholas Lemann, "Bush's Trillions," *New Yorker* (February 19, 2001).

Est modus in rebus, sunt certi denique fines, / quos ultra citraque nequit consistere rectum.

There is a mean in all things and, moreover, set limits on either side of which right cannot exist.

—Horace, *Sat.* 1.1.106.

Modus omnibus in rebus, soror, optumum est habitu; / nimia omnia nimium exhibent negoti hominibus ex se.

In everything moderation is best thing to have, sister: all things in excess bring excessive trouble to people.

–Plautus, *Poen.* 238–39.

He knows to live who keeps the middle state, and neither leans on this side nor on that.

–Alexander Pope, "The Second Satire of the Second Book of Horace," 61 (1733–38).

Time

 χρόνον δ' ἔγνων ὃν παρῆλθον, / ὃν ἔχω δραμεῖν οὐκ οἶδα.

I know the time I've passed through, but not what I have yet to run.

–Anacreontea 40.3–4 (Loeb, *Greek Lyric II*).

χρόνος . . . πενθέων φάρμακα μοῦνος ἔχει.

Only time has the cure for sorrow.

–Philetas, quoted in Stobaeus 124.26.

The woods are lovely, dark and deep. / But I have promises to keep, / and miles to go before I sleep.

–Robert Frost, "Stopping by Woods on a Snowy Evening" (1923).

 πάλιν χρόνῳ τἀρχαῖα καινὰ γίγνεται.

With time everything becomes new again.

–Nicostratus, frag 3 (*FCG*).

Don't throw the past away, you might need it some rainy day. Dreams can come true again, when everything old is new again.

–Carole Bayer Sager and Peter Woolnough Allen, "Everything Old Is New Again," song in *All That Jazz* (1979).

🏛 Fugit hora.

Time flies.

–Persius 5.153.

Time flies.

–Popular saying.

Tolerance

 ὁ ὅμοιος τῷ ὁμοίῳ
Like unto like

> –Plato, *Grg.* 510b.

Suum cuique pulchrum est.
To each his own is beautiful.

> –Cicero, *Tusc.* 5.63.

To each his own

> –Popular saying

 δύο λόγους εἶναι περὶ παντὸς
πράγματος.
[He said] that there are two opinions on everything.

> –Protagoras, quoted in Diogenes Laertius
> 9.8.51.

There are two sides to every story.

> –Popular saying.

Travel

🏛 **Viam qui nescit qua deveniat ad mare, / eum oportet amnem quaerere comitem sibi.**

If someone doesn't know the way to the sea, he should seek out a stream as his companion.
–Plautus, *Poen.* 627–28.

Say you are in the country; in some high land
   of lakes. Take almost any path you please,
   and ten to one it carries you down in a dale,
   and leaves you there by a pool in the stream.
   . . . Let the most absent-minded of men be
   plunged in his deepest reveries—stand that
   man on his legs, set his feet a-going, and he
   will infallibly lead you to water, if water there
   be in all that region.
–Herman Melville, *Moby Dick*, ch. 1
   (1851).

🏛 **Caelum, non animum mutant, qui trans mare currunt.**

Those who travel across the sea change their sky, not their mind.
–Horace, *Sat.* 1.11.27.

*Wherever You Go, There You Are: Mindfulness
   Meditation in Everyday Life*
–Jon Kabat-Zinn, title of book (2014).

Comes facundus in via pro vehiculo est.

A witty companion upon the road is as good as a vehicle.
–Publilius Syrus 116.

Good company in a journey makes the way to seem the shorter.
–Izaak Walton, *The Compleat Angler* (1653).

True or False?

 ἁπλᾶ γάρ ἐστι τῆς ἀληθείας ἔπη.

Simple are the words of truth.

–Aeschylus, *Oedipus* frag. 176.

Veritatis enim absolutio semper est simplex.

Perfect truth is always simple.

–Ammianus Marcellinus 14.10.13.

The plain, unvarnished truth

–Popular saying.

Give it to me straight.

–Popular saying.

 οὐδὲν ἔρπει ψεῦδος εἰς γῆρας χρόνου.

No lie creeps into old age.

–Sophocles, *Acrisius* frag. 62.

ψευδόμενος οὐδεὶς λανθάνει πολὺν χρόνον.

No liar goes undetected for long.

–Menander, *Mon.* 547.

ἀδύνατον ὡς ἔοικε, τἀληθὲς λαθεῖν.

It seems impossible for the truth to lie hidden.

–Menander, quoted in Stobaeus 76.19 (= frag. 823, *CAF*).

ἔρχεται τἀληθὲς εἰς φῶς ἐνίοτ' οὐ
ζητούμενον.

The truth occasionally comes to light, even if unsought.
−Menander, frag. 433 (*CAF*).

But at the length, truth will / out.
−William Shakespeare, *Merchant of Venice*, act 2 scene 2 (1596–97).

🏛 Verumque est illud quod vulgo dicitur, mendacem memorem esse oportere.

The common saying is true—a liar should have a good memory.
−Quintilian 4.2.91.

Liars need not have long memories if they address themselves only to fools, who have short ones.
−A. E. Housman, preface to *M. Manilii Astronomicon, Liber Tertius* (1937).

🏛 Quod dare non possis, verbis promittere noli.

Don't promise with words what you can't give.
−Cato, *Dist.* 1.25.

Miss Ritter: Peter, don't make promises you can't keep.

Peter Parker: Yeah, but those are the best kind.
−Barbara Eve Harris playing Miss Ritter and Andrew Garfield playing Peter Parker in *The Amazing Spider-Man*, film (2012). Screenplay by James Vanderbilt, Alvin Sargent, and Steve Kloves.

Vanity

🏛 **Adulatio, perpetuum malum regum**

Praise, the eternal bane of kings

–Quintus Curtius 8.5.6.

Trahimur omnes studio laudis et optimus quisque maxime gloria ducitur.

We are all motivated by a desire for praise and even the noblest man is greatly led on by the desire for fame.

–Cicero, *Arch.* 26.

They do abuse the king that flatter him: / for flattery is the bellows blows up sin.

–William Shakespeare, *Pericles, Prince of Tyre*, act 1 scene 2 (ca. 1607–8).

Virtue

 ἀναφαίρετον ὅπλον ἡ ἀρετή.

Moral excellence is a weapon that cannot be taken away.

—Antisthenes, quoted in Diogenes
Laertius 6.1.12.

But they cannot take away our self-respect if we do not give it to them.

—Spoken by Ben Kingsley playing
Mahatma Gandhi in *Gandhi*, film
(1982). Screenplay by John Briley.

 Ipsa quidem virtus sibimet pulcherrima merces.

Virtue is indeed a most beautiful reward for itself.

—Silius Italicus 13.663.

Ipsa quidem virtus pretium sibi.

Virtue itself is its own reward.

—Claudian, *De Consulatu Manlii Theodori* 1.

Virtue is its own reward.

—Popular saying.

War & Peace

War

🏛 οὐκ ἔστιν ἐν πολέμῳ δὶς ἁμαρτεῖν.

There is no making a mistake twice in war.
                                    –Plutarch, *Apoph. bas.* 186f.

The unwritten motto of United States Robot and Mechanical Men Corp. was well-known: "No employee makes the same mistake twice. He is fired the first time."
                                    –Isaac Asimov, *I Robot* (1950).

🏛 **Silent leges inter arma.**

In wartime laws are silent.
                                    –Cicero, *Mil.* 11.

All's fair in love and war.
                                    –Popular saying.

🏛 ἔστιν ὁ πόλεμος οὐχ ὅπλων τὸ πλέον,
   ἀλλὰ δαπάνης, δι' ἣν τὰ ὅπλα ὠφελεῖ.

War is, for the most part, not a matter of arms, but of money, which helps procure the arms.
                                    –Thucydides 1.83.2.

Nervi belli pecunia infinita.

An infinite amount money is the sinews of war.
                                    –Cicero, *Phil.* 5.5.

The world in arms is not spending money
alone. It is spending the sweat of its laborers,
the genius of its scientists, the hopes of its
children.

> –Dwight D. Eisenhower, speech to the
> American Society of Newspaper
> Editors (April 16, 1953).

🏛 οὐδὲ λύκοι τε καὶ ἄρνες ὁμόφρονα
θυμὸν ἔχουσιν.

Wolves and sheep do not have like-minded spirits.
> –Homer, *Il.* 22.263.

The lion and the calf shall lie down together, but
the calf won't get much sleep.

> –Woody Allen, "Scrolls," *The New
> Republic* (August 31, 1974).

Peace

🏛 Qui desiderat pacem, praeparet
bellum.

Let one who desires peace prepare for war.
> –Vegetius, prologue 3.

Si pace frui volumus, bellum gerendum
est.

If we wish to enjoy peace, then war must be waged.
> –Cicero, *Phil.* 7.19.

The best defense is a good offense.
> –Popular saying.

Wise & Foolish

🏛 **κρεῖττον σιωπᾶν ἐστιν ἢ λαλεῖν μάτην.**

It's better to be silent than babble meaninglessly.

> –Variously attributed to Philonides (frag. 17, *CAF*) or Menander (frag. 409, Jäkel).

Taciturnitas stulto homini pro sapientia est.

Quietness is taken as wisdom in a stupid person.
> –Publilius Syrus 693.

Better to remain silent and be thought a fool than to speak and to remove all doubt.
> –Attributed, incorrectly, to Abraham Lincoln or Mark Twain.

🏛 ## Quod flumen placidum est, forsan latet altius unda.

Perhaps the water lies deeper where the river is smooth.
> –Cato, *Dist.* 4.31.

Still waters run deep.
> –Popular saying.

🏛 ## Qui stultis videri eruditi volunt stulti eruditis videntur.

Those who wish to seem learned to fools seem fools to the learned.
> –Quintilian 10.7.22.

οἱ γὰρ ἐν σοφοῖς / φαῦλοι παρ' ὄχλῳ
μουσικώτεροι λέγειν.

For those who seem foolish to the wise are fairly inspired
speakers to a crowd.

–Euripides, *Hipp.* 989–90.

He was a man of the world among men of
letters, a man of letters among men of the
world.

–Thomas Babington Macaulay, review
of Courtenay's *Memoirs of the*
Life, Works and Correspondence
of Sir William Temple, printed in
the *Edinburgh Review* (October
1838), reprinted in *Literary Essays:*
Contributed to the Edinburgh Review
by Lord Macaulay (1932).

Parva leves capiunt animos.

Trifling things seize flighty minds.

–Ovid, *Ars* 1.159.

I am astonished to observe how willing men are
to lumber their minds with such rubbish—to
permit idle rumors and incidents of the most
insignificant kind to intrude on ground which
should be sacred to thought.

–Henry David Thoreau, "Life without
Principle" (1863).

Quae nimis apparent retia, vitat avis.

If the nets are too obvious, the bird avoids them.

–Ovid, *Rem.* 516.

οὐκ οἷόν τε ἁπαλὸν τυρὸν ἀγκίστρῳ
ἐπισπᾶσθαι.

You can't snag soft cheese with a hook.

–Bion, quoted in Diogenes Laertius 4.7.48.

You catch more flies with honey than with
vinegar.

–Popular saying.

🏛 **Fundum alienum arat, incultum
familiarem deserit.**

He plows another man's land and leaves his own untilled.

–Plautus, *Asin.* 874. The metaphor is
sexual in nature.

My own business always bores me to death. I
prefer other people's.

–Oscar Wilde, *Lady Windermere's Fan,*
act 3 (1892).

🏛 ἐπὶ ῥιπὸς πλεῖν

To sail on a raft of straw

–Ancient proverb, giving an example of
foolish behavior; cf. Euripides, *Thyestes*
frag. 397 (κἂν ἐπὶ ῥιπὸς πλέοις, "Even
if you sailed on a straw mat") and
Aristophanes, *Pax* 699 (κέρδους ἕκατι
κἂν ἐπὶ ῥιπὸς πλέοι, "He'd sail on a
straw mat for a profit").

Wynken, Blynken, and Nod one night / sailed
off in a wooden shoe— / Sailed on a river of
crystal light / into a sea of dew.

–Eugene Field, "Wynken, Blynken, and
Nod" (1889).

Insanus omnis furere credit ceteros.

Every crazy person thinks everyone else is crazy.

–Publilius Syrus, in some collections.

Just because you're paranoid it doesn't mean they're not out to get you.

–Popular saying, misattributed to Joseph Heller's *Catch-22*; famous to some from lyrics on the band Nirvana's album *Never Mind* (1991).

 πολλοῖς γὰρ ἡ γλῶττα προτρέχει τῆς διανοίας.

In many the tongue outruns the thought process.

–Isocrates, *Dem.* 41.

The facts were constantly outrunning his thoughts.

–Henry Adams, *The Education of Henry Adams*, ch. 22 (1907).

Work

🏛 ὅς οἱ πολλὰ καμῃσι, θεὸς δ' ἐπὶ ἔργον
   ἀέξῃ.

*God causes the work of one who works hard for himself to
prosper.*

–Homer, *Od.* 14.65.

A man who works at another's will, not for his
own passion or his own need, but for money
or honor, is always a fool.

–Johann Wolfgang von Goethe, *The
Sorrows of Young Werther* (English
trans., 1779).

🏛 **Leve fit, quod bene fertur, onus.**

A burden that is carried well becomes light.

–Ovid, *Am.* 1.2.10.

The reward of a thing well done, is to have done it.

–Ralph Waldo Emerson, "New England
Reformers: Lecture at Amory Hall,"
Essays: Second Series (1844).

🏛 **Non quia difficilia sunt, non
   audemus, sed quia non audemus,
   difficilia sunt.**

*It is not because things are difficult that we don't dare to do
them; rather, they are difficult because we don't dare.*

–Seneca, *EM* 104.26.

Non est ad astra mollis e terris via.

The path from earth to the stars is not easy.

–Seneca, *Herc. F.* 437.

We choose to go to the Moon in this decade and
do the other things, not because they are easy,
but because they are hard.

–John F. Kennedy, speech at Rice
University (September 12, 1962).

🏛 Adeo facilius est multa facere quam diu.

It is much easier to do many things, than [a single one] for a long time.

–Quintilian 1.12.7.

Jack of all trades, master of none

–Popular saying.

World Around Us

🏛 **Mihi contuenti se persuasit rerum natura nihil incredibile existimare de ea.**

As I contemplated her, Nature has persuaded me to think that nothing about her is incredible.

−Pliny the Elder 11.6.

The world will never starve for want of wonders; but only for want of wonder.

−G. K. Chesterton, *Tremendous Trifles* (1909).

🏛 **οὐδὲν γὰρ, ὡς φαμὲν, μάτην ἡ φύσις ποιεῖ.**

For, as we say, nature does nothing in vain.

−Aristotle, *Pol.* 1253a.

Naturam expelles furca, tamen usque recurret, / et mala perrumpet furtim fastidia victrix.

You can drive nature out with a pitchfork, but it will still reappear and, as a victor, will stealthily break through your nasty scorn.

−Horace, *Epist.* 1.10.24−25. Horace is debating the merits of life in the country versus that in the city with his friend Fuscus. The contempt Horace mentions is that of believing that one can plant trees and shrubs in a city and think it as good as the

country. The poet Martial believed
they were not mutually exclusive and
said, "Rus in urbe" (A countryside in
the city; *Epig.* 12.57.21).

Scientific research is based on the assumption
that all events, including the actions of
mankind, are determined by the laws of
nature.

–Albert Einstein, letter to sixth grade
student Phyllis Wright (January 24,
1936), quoted in Max Jammer, *Einstein
and Religion: Physics and Theology*
(1999).

Writing

🏛 **Brevis esse laboro, / obscurus fio.**
I struggle to be brief, and I become vague.
　　　　　–Horace, *Ars P.* 24–25.

I have made this letter longer than usual, only
　　because I have not had time to make it
　　shorter.

> –Blaise Pascal, letter (1657); often
> misattributed to Mark Twain, who
> undoubtedly wished he had said it.
> Twain did say, in a letter to James
> Redpath (June 15, 1871), "The reason
> I dread writing letters is because I am
> so apt to get to slinging wisdom &
> forget to let up. Thus much precious
> time is lost."

🏛 **Verbum omne, quod non intellectum
adiuvat, neque ornatum, vitiosum
dici potest.**
*Every word that aids neither understanding nor ornamentation
can be called flawed.*
　　　　　–Quintilian 8.3.55.

The difference between the almost right word
　　and the right word is really a large matter—
　　'tis the difference between the lightning-bug
　　and the lightning.

> –Mark Twain, letter to George Bainton
> (October 15, 1888).

Youth

 At tu, dum primi floret tibi temporis aetas, / utere. Non tardo labitur illa pede.

But you, as long as the prime of your life is in full bloom, use it! It is slipping away at no small pace.

–Tibullus 1.8.47–48.

Ne pereant lege mane rosas: cito virgo senescit.

Pick roses in the morning, lest they die: a young girl soon grows old.

–Florus, *On the Quality of Life* 11.9.

Gather ye Rose-buds while ye may, / old Time is still a-flying; / and this same flower that smiles to-day, / tomorrow will be dying.

–Robert Herrick, "To the Virgins, to Make Much of Time" (1648).

 Facile est enim teneros adhuc animos componere; difficulter reciduntur vitia quae nobiscum creverunt.

It is easy to mold spirits while they are still young; vices that have grown up with us are pruned with difficulty.

–Seneca, *Ira* 2.18.2.

As the twig is bent, so grows the tree.

–Popular saying.

🏛 ἤβης ἀγλαὸν ἄνθος

The shining/spendid flower of youth
> –Theognis 1008.

The bloom of youth
> –Popular saying.

🏛 νέα γὰρ φροντὶς οὐκ ἀλγεῖν φιλεῖ.

A young head does not like to grieve.
> –Euripides, *Med.* 48.

Youth's the season made for joys.
> –John Gay, *The Beggar's Opera*, act 2 scene
> 4, air 22.

Proverbs & Sayings

There does not seem to be a single word for the time-worn sayings every culture possesses: adage, aphorism, apothegm, byword, epigram, maxim, proverb, saw, saying, sententia (directly from the Latin). But when we see such things, we immediately recognize them. They are old and shopworn. They are gnarled and short, like a grouchy old man shooing children away from his apple tree. And they are long lived, passed down through the ages by grandparents, parents, and, in general, elders. Why? Because they all contain a germ of truth. What follows is a selection of such sayings that do not readily fall into a single category. Use with caution. Your children will tire of hearing them until they repeat them to their own children.

Note: This section lists proverbs and sayings in English alphabetical order. Many sayings are given as parallels to examples offered elsewhere in this book.

A cobbler should stick to his last.

Ne supra crepidam sutor iudicaret.

A cobbler should make no judgment other than on a sandal.

> –Pliny the Elder 35.85. The famous painter Apelles (contemporary of Alexander the Great), after finishing a painting, used to hang them for public view and privately listen to viewers' comments. A cobbler caught him out one day for incorrectly depicting a sandal. But when he came back later and criticized a leg, he was met with this rejoinder.

🏛 A word to the wise is sufficient.

Dictum sapienti sat est.

A word to the wise is enough.

–Plautus, *Per.* 729; Terence, *Phorm.* 541;
SHA, *Tac.* 19.5.

🏛 Actions speak louder than words.

τὰ γὰρ ἔργα οἶμαί σοι πιθανώτερα παρεσχῆσθαι τῶν νῦν λεχθέντων λόγων.

I think my actions tell you more about the matter than the words just spoken.

–Xenophon, *Cyr.* 6.4.5. Panthea, to her husband Abradatas (an ally of the Persian king Cyrus the Great), when she had pawned her jewelry to buy him appropriate armor.

🏛 Add fuel to the fire.

Adde cruorem / stultitiae, atque ignem gladio scrutare.

Add blood to stupidity and stir the fire with a sword.

–Horace, *Sat.* 2.3.275–76.

Oleum adde camino.

Add oil to the furnace.

–Horace, *Sat.* 2.3.321.

🏛 Add insult to injury.

Ad damnum adderetur iniuria.
Injury was added to ruin.
> –Cicero, *Tul.* 17.41.

Iniuriae qui addideris contumeliam.
You, who have added insult to injury.
> –Phaedrus 5.3.5.

🏛 After three days, fish and guests stink.

Hospes nullus tam in amici hospitium divorti potest, / quin, ubi triduum continuum fuerit, iam odiosus siet.
No guest can partake of a friend's hospitality for three straight days without becoming odious.
> –Plautus, *Mil.* 741–42

🏛 Apples and oranges

ἐγὼ σκόροδά σοι λέγω, σὺ δὲ κρόμμυ' ἀποκρίνεις.
I'm talking to you about garlic and you give me an answer about onions.
> –Frag. of a lost comedy (?); preserved in von Leutsch 48a and Erasmus, *Adages* 5.2335 (Lisdonk).

🏛 ## As useful as lips on a chicken
(with other, less subtle variants)

Clitellae bovi sunt impositae.
Pack saddles have been put on an ox.
−Cicero, *Att.* 108.3.

🏛 ## Beggars can't be choosers.

κακὸς δ' αἰδοῖος ἀλήτης.
A bashful beggar is a bad one.
−Homer, *Od.* 17.578.

🏛 ## Belt and suspenders

Taetra enim res est . . . velis, ut ita dicam, remisque fugienda.
It's a foul business . . . and must be fled from with both sails and oars, so to speak.
−Cicero, *Tusc.* 3.25.

🏛 ## Better late than never

Potiusque sero quam nunquam
Late rather than never
−Livy 4.2.11.

🏛 ## Better the devil you know than the one you don't

Nota mala res optima est.
A bad thing that's known is the best sort.
−Plautus, *Trin.* 63.

Notissimum quodque malum maxime tolerabile.

The evil that is best known is the most bearable.

–Livy 23.3.

🏛 Better to wear out than rust out

Vita humana prope uti ferrum est. Si exerceas, conteritur; si non exerceas, tamen rubigo interficit.

Human life is rather like iron. If you use it, it wears out; if, however, you don't use it, rust still does it in.

–Cato the Elder, quoted in Aulus Gellius 11.2.6.

🏛 Between a rock and a hard place

Nunc ego omnino occidi, nunc ego inter sacrum saxumque sto, nec quid faciam scio.

Now I'm totally dead! I'm standing betweeen the altar and the knife. And I don't know what to do.

–Plautus, *Capt.* 616.

🏛 Call a spade a spade

τὰ σῦκα σῦκα, τὴν σκάφην δὲ σκάφην ὀνομάσων

Calling a fig a fig, a tub a tub

–The words as quoted come from Lucian, *Hist. conscr.* 41, himself quoting "a certain writer of comedies." The real author is unknown but has been said to be Aristophanes or even Menander.

Although the word σκάφην is secure (cf. Plutarch, *Apoph. bas.* 178B) and means "tub" or "trough," Erasmus (*Adages* 3.1205) misread it as σπάθην and translated it into Latin as *ligonem*, "shovel." From there it became "spade" and is so quoted today.

ἔφη φύσει καὶ ἀγροίκους εἶναι Μακεδόνας καὶ τὴν σκάφην σκάφην λέγοντας.

He [King Philip] said that Macedonians are country folk by nature and that they call a tub a tub.

–Plutarch, *Apoph. bas.* 178b.

🏛 Calm after the storm

εὐδίαι γὰρ ἐκ μεγάλαν ἀήταν / αἶψα πέλονται.

Periods of calm occur right after great storms.

–Sappho, newly discovered frag. of a poem called "The Brothers," 11–12.

🏛 Can't fill someone's shoes

οὔτε τὰ τοῦ Ἀχιλλέως ὅπλα τῷ Θερσίτῃ ... ἁρμόττει.

Achilles's armor doesn't fit Thersites.

–Attributed to Socrates in Stobaeus 4.118 and to the Pythagoreans (Elter, 80). Achilles was the greatest hero of the *Iliad*; Thersites was the ugliest and vilest soldier before Troy, who, in book 1, reviles Agamemnon only to receive a beating and derision in return.

🏛 Can't have your cake and eat it too

Non tibi illud apparere, si sumas, potest / nisi tu immortale rere esse argentum tibi.

That [your money] can't still be there if you spend it—unless you think it is immortal.

–Plautus, *Trin.* 414–15.

🏛 Can't see the forest for the trees

Tardi ingenii est rivulos consectari, fontis rerum non videre.

It is a sign of dull-wittedness to follow tiny streams, but not to see the sources of things.

–Cicero, *De Orat.* 2.117.

μῆ νῦν τὰ πόρσω, τἀγγύθεν μεθεὶς, σκόπει.

Don't look now at far off things while missing the things close by.

–Euripides, *Rhes.* 482.

🏛 Children should be seen and not heard.

Plus oportet scire servom quam loqui.

A slave should know more than he says.

–Plautus, *Mil.* 477.

🏛 Conspicuous by their absence

> Viginti clarissimarum familiarum imagines antelatae sunt . . . sed praefulgebant Cassius atque Brutus eo ipso quod effigies eorum non visebantur.

The busts from twenty most illustrious families were carried in the procession . . . but Cassius and Brutus were the most prominent by the very fact that their likenesses were not to be seen.

–Tacitus, *Ann.* 3.76. Junia Tertia, wife of one of the assassins of Julius Caesar, omitted the emperor Tiberius in her will. He still approved her funeral procession, but without the family busts of her husband and his fellow assassin.

🏛 Counting your chickens before they hatch

> πρὸ τῆς νίκης τὸ ἐγκώμιον ᾄδεις.

You're singing the victory song before the victory.

–Diogenianus 7.56.

🏛 Diamonds are forever.

> κτῆμά τε ἐς ἀεί

A possession for all time

–Thucydides 1.22.4, quoting Pericles's Funeral Oration.

🏛 Die like a dog

θάνατος μὲν οὖν κύνειος
A dog's death

> –Aristophanes, *Vesp.* 898.

🏛 Dirt cheap

Itaque illo tempore annona pro luto erat.
At that time, you could get grain for mud.

> –Petronius 44; the character Ganymede
> is longing for the good old days.

🏛 Don't judge a book by its cover.

Frontis nulla fides.
There is no faith in a forehead.

> –Juvenal 2.8. In other words, don't trust
> appearances.

Saepe est etiam sub palliolo sordido sapientia.
Wisdom often lies beneath a dirty cloak.

> –Cicero, citing Caecilius Statius, *Tusc.*
> 3.56.

🏛 Don't kill the messenger.

στέργει γὰρ οὐδεὶς ἄγγελον κακῶν ἐπῶν.
No one loves a messenger of bad news.

> –Sophocles, *Ant.* 277.

🏛 Don't make the same mistake twice.

δὶς πρὸς τὸν αὐτὸν αἰσχρὸν προσκρούειν
λίθον.

It's a disgrace to stumble on the same stone twice.
—Proverbial, sometimes attributed to
Zenodotus.

🏛 Easy come easy go

Male partum, male disperit.

Ill got, ill lost.
—Plautus, *Poen.* 844.

🏛 Eyes in the back of his head

**[Anus] quae in occipitio quoque habet
oculos pessima.**

*An old woman who has eyes on the back of her head as well
is the worst kind.*
—Plautus, *Aul.* 64.

🏛 Fake it till you make it.

Possunt quia posse videntur.

They have strength because they look like they have it.
—Vergil, *Aen.* 5.231.

🏛 **Fish out of water**

ὥσπερ οἱ ἰχθύες ἐγχρονίζοντες τῇ ξηρᾷ
τελευτῶσιν οὕτως καὶ οἱ μοναχοὶ
βραδύνοντες ἔξω τοῦ χελλίου.

*Just as fish that are on dry land too long die, so do monks
loitering outside their cell.*

> –"Athanasius's Life of Antony,"
> *Apophthegmata Patrum* (Migne
> 77.27).

🏛 **Fitting a square peg into a round hole**

οἱ ἔμπαλιν ὑποδούμενοι παραλλάξας

Those who put their sandals on the wrong feet
> –Plato, *Tht.* 193c.

🏛 **Forbidden fruit**

**Quod licet, ingratum est, quod non licet,
acrius urit.**

What is allowed is not welcome, what is not burns the hotter.
> –Ovid, *Am.* 2.19.3.

🏛 **Grass is always greener in the other
fellow's yard (*or* on the other side of
the fence).**

οὐδέ σ' ἀρέσκει τὸ παρόν, τὸ δ' ἀπὸν
φίλτερον ἡγῇ.

*What is right here does not please you; instead you think
what is absent is dearer.*
> –Euripides, *Hipp.* 184–85.

Aliena nobis, nostra plus aliis placent.

Others' things are pleasing to us, ours are more pleasing to others.

−Publilius Syrus 28.

Nulli ad aliena respicienti sua placent.

No one looking over the possessions of others is happy with his own.

−Seneca, *Ira* 3.31.1.

Fertilior seges est alienis semper in agris; / vicinumque pecus grandius uber habet.

The grain is always more fertile in someone else's fields; a neighbor's cow has the bigger udder.

−Ovid, *Ars* 1.349–50.

🏛 Haste makes waste.

In tumultu festinatio quoque tarda est.

Amid confusion, even haste is slow.

−Quintus Curtius 9.9.12, describing a chaotic retreat from the battlefield.

🏛 Hindsight is 20/20.

κἀν βροτοῖς / αἱ δεύτεραί πως φροντίδες σοφώτεραι.

Among mortals, second thoughts are somehow wiser.

−Euripides, *Hipp.* 435–36.

Posteriores enim cogitationes, ut aiunt, sapientiores solent esse.

Later thoughts, as they say, are usually wiser ones.

–Cicero, *Phil.* 12.5.

🏛 **Hoist on my own petard.**

(Commonly misquoted, using "hoisted," from William Shakespeare, *Hamlet*, act 3 scene 4, "For 'tis the sport to have the engineer / Hoist with his own petard.")

Patior telis vulnera facta meis!

I'm suffering wounds made by my own weapons!

–Ovid, *Her.* 2.48.

🏛 **I have no dog in this fight.**

Mihi istic nec seritur nec metitur.

There is neither sowing nor reaping for me there.

–Plautus, *Epid.* 265.

🏛 **Idle hands are the devil's playground.**

Fac et aliquid operis, ut semper te diabolus inveniat occupatum.

And do a bit of work, so that the devil will always find you occupied.

–St. Jerome, *Ep.* 125.11.

🏛 Ignorance is bliss.

κέρδος δ' ἐν κακοῖς ἀγνωσία.
Ignorance amid evils is an advantage.
–Euripides, *Antiope* frag. 205.

Certe ignoratio futurorum malorum utilior est quam scientia.
Certainly ignorance of future evils is more useful than knowledge of them.
–Cicero, *Div.* 2.23.

🏛 In one ear and out the other

Neque solum haec ipse debebit docere praeceptor, sed frequenter interrogare et iudicium discipulorum experiri. Sic audientibus securitas aberit nec quae dicentur superfluent aures.
The teacher himself will not only teach these things but will frequently ask questions and test the judgment of his students. In this way, he can be sure that the things that will be said will not flow past their ears.
–Quintilian 2.5.13.

🏛 Jumping to conclusions

ἐξ ὀνύχος τὸν λέοντα γράφοντας
Painting a lion from its claw
–Alcaeus, quoted in Plutarch, *De def. or.*
3. This phrase became proverbial for making conclusions based on too little evidence.

🏛 **Keep your eyes on the prize.**

κατὰ Σόλωνα δὲ χρεὼν τέλος ὁρᾶν;
Must we, following Solon, keep the goal in sight?
–Aristotle, *Eth. Nic.* 1100a.

🏛 **Laughter is the best medicine.**

Humanius est deridere vitam quam deplorare.
It more genteel to laugh at life than to moan about it.
–Seneca, *Tranq.* 15.2.

🏛 **Leave no stone unturned.**

πάντα κινῆσαι πέτρον
To move every stone
–Euripides, *Heracl.* 1002.

🏛 **Like attracts like.**

ἀεὶ τὸ ὅμοιον ὂν ὅμοιον παρακαλεῖ.
Like always summons like.
–Plato, *Resp.* 425c.

🏛 **Like father, like son**

Qualis dominus, talis et servus
As the master, so the slave
–Petronius 58.

🏛 Live to fight another day

Qui fugiebat, rursus proeliabitur.
The one who was fleeing will fight again.
> –Tertullian, *On Flight from Persecution* 10.

🏛 Look before you leap.

**ὑπὸ παντὶ λίθῳ σκορπίον ὦ ἑταῖρε
φυλάσσεο.**
*Watch out for the scorpion, my friend, that is under every
stone.*
> –Praxilla, frag. 750. Aristophanes played
> on this line and said, "I agree with the
> old proverb that we should look under
> every rock lest we be bitten by—a
> politician!" (*Thesm.* 528–30).

🏛 Make a mountain out of a molehill

ἐλέφαντα ἐκ μυίας ποιεῖν
To make an elephant out of a fly
> –Lucian, *The Fly* 12.

Arcem ex cloaca facere
To make a citadel out of a sewer
> –Cicero, *Planc.* 95; *arcem* is sometimes
> given as *arcum*, a triumphal arch.

Si aut tragoedias agamus in nugis
Or if we were to make tragedies out of trifles
> –Cicero, *De Orat.* 2.205.

🏛 Method to his madness

Insanire ... certa ratione modoque

To go mad with a fixed reason and method
                    –Horace, *Sat.* 2.3.271.

🏛 Might makes right.

Non recte suadetis, familiares, qui non patimini me illum doctiorem omnibus credere, qui habet triginta legiones.

You give poor advice, my friends, when you do not allow me to consider the one with thirty legions to be the smarter one.

> –*SHA, Hadr.* 15.13. A rhetorician had not argued with Hadrian on the proper use of a word even though the emperor was demonstrably wrong. The rhetorician made this reply to his friends, who urged him to argue the point.

🏛 Mind your own business.

αἰσχρὸν τὰ ὀθνεῖα πολυπραγμονέοντα ἀγνοεῖν τὰ οἰκεῖα.

It is shameful to poke your nose into other people's business and not know what is going on in your own house.
                    –Democritus, frag. 80 (D-K).

🏛 Nip it in the bud.

Flamma recens parva sparsa resedit aqua.

A new flame settles down at a little sprinkle of water.
—Ovid, *Her.* 17.190.

🏛 No pain, no gain

τὴν μέν τοι Κακότητα καὶ ἰλαδὸν ἔστιν ἐλέσθαι / ῥηιδίως· λείη μὲν ὁδός, μάλα δ᾽ ἐγγύθι ναίει· / τῆς δ᾽ Ἀρετῆς ἱδρῶτα θεοὶ προπάροιθεν ἔθηκαν / ἀθάνατοι.

Now, it is easy to snatch Misery by the bunches, because that road is smooth, and she lives quite close. But the immortal gods have placed sweat in front of Excellence.
—Hesiod, *Op.* 286–90.

πόνου τοι χωρὶς οὐδὲν εὐτυχεῖ.

Indeed, without pain there is no success.
—Sophocles, *El.* 945.

τὸ λεγόμενον ἀληθές, ὅτι χαλεπὰ τὰ καλά.

The saying is true: good things are hard.
—Plato, *Resp.* 435c.

Necesse est facere sumptum, qui quaerit lucrum.

One who seeks profit has to incur some expense.
—Plautus, *Asin.* 217.

Non fit sine periclo facinus magnum et memorabile.

No great and memorable deed comes to be without some danger.

–Terence, *Heaut.* 314.

Nil sine magno / vita labore dedit mortalibus.

Life has given nothing to mortals without great labor.

–Horace, *Sat.* 1.9.58–59.

🏛 Not to give a tinker's dam

Ego non flocci pendere.

I didn't value it as much as a piece of fluff.

–Terence, *Eun.* 411.

🏛 Nothing in common

Nihil cum fidibus graculost, nihil cum amaracino sui.

The jackdaw has no use for a lyre, or a pig for face cream.

–Proverb cited by Aulus Gellius, preface 19.

🏛 Now or never

Qui non est hodie, cras minus aptus erit.

Who isn't ready today will be less ready tomorrow.

–Ovid, *Rem.* 94.

🏛 Nowhere to go but up

Fortuna miserrima tuta est, / nam timor eventus deterioris abest.

Even the most wretched misfortune is safe because the fear of a worse event is absent.

–Ovid, *Pont.* 2.2.31–32.

🏛 One bad apple can spoil the barrel.

Sincerum est nisi vas, quodcumque infundis acescit.

If the pot isn't clean, whatever you pour in goes bad.

–Horace, *Epist.* 1.2.54.

🏛 One damned thing after another

Aliud ex alio malum.

One bad thing comes from another.

–Terence, *Eun.* 987.

🏛 One swallow doesn't make a summer.

Fallimur? An veris praenuntia venit hirundo?

Are we deceived? Or has the swallow, the harbinger of spring, come?

–Ovid, *Fast.* 2.853.

🏛 Out of the frying pan, into the fire

"De fumo," ut aiunt, "ad flammam."
As people say, "Out of the smoke, toward the flame."
> –Ammianus Marcellinus 28.1.26; cf. 14.11.12.

🏛 Practice makes perfect.

μελέτη τὸ πᾶν.
Practice is everything.
> –Periander of Corinth, quoted in Diogenes Laertius 1.7.99.

🏛 Put the cart before the horse

ἡ ἄμαξα τὸν βοῦν πολλάκις ἐκφέρει.
The cart often draws the ox.
> –Lucian, *Dial. mort.* 349.

🏛 Putty in your hands

Argilla quidvis imitaberis uda.
Out of the wet clay that he is, you'll shape him into whatever you want.
> –Horace, *Epist.* 2.2.8.

🏛 Ramrod straight (British) / Stick up his butt (American)

τί οὖν ἡμῖν ὀβελίσκον καταπιὼν περιπατεῖς;

Why, then, do you walk around like you had swallowed a barbecue spit?

–Epictetus, *Discourses* 1.21.

🏛 Rare bird

Rara avis

A rare bird

–Persius 1.46, referring to a rare happening.

Corvo quoque rarior albo

Rarer than a white crow

–Juvenal 7.202.

Rara avis in terris, nigroque simillima cycno

A rare bird in the lands, very like a black swan

–Juvenal 6.165.

🏛 Rats desert a sinking ship.

Ruinis inminentibus musculi praemigrant.

When buildings are about to fall down, the mice move out first.

–Pliny the Elder 8.103.

🏛 Reap what you sow

Ut sementem feceris ita metes.

As you have sown, so will you reap.

> –Marcus Pinarius Rusca, cited by Cicero, *De Orat.* 2.261.

🏛 Same old song

Cantilenam eandem canis.

You're singing the same tune.

> –Terence, *Phorm.* 491.

🏛 Second to none

Nulli secundus

Second to nothing/no one

> –Apuleius, *Flor.* 9.15.

🏛 Semper paratus

(Always prepared—Coast Guard's motto)

Breve tempus longum est imparatis.

A short time is long for the unprepared.

> –Cicero, *Phil.* 3.2.

🏛 Skin and bones

Ossa atque pellis sum miser a macritudine.

I am a wretch, bones and skin, from this thinness.

> –Plautus, *Capt.* 135.

🏛 Slippery as an eel

Anguilla est, elabitur!
He's an eel—he's slipping away!
    –Plautus, *Pseud.* 747.

🏛 Snail's pace

Podagrosi estis ac vicistis cochleam tarditudine.
You've got gout and have defeated the snail in slowness.
    –Plautus, *Poen.* 532.

🏛 Sour grapes

ὄμφαξ ὁ βότρυς, οὐ πέπειρος, ὡς ᾤμην.
The grapes are sour, not ripe, as I thought.
    –Aesop, preserved in Babrius 19.8.

🏛 Still waters run deep.

Saepe summa ingenia in occulto latent.
Great talents often lie in hiding.
    –Plautus, *Capt.* 165.

🏛 Taken with a grain of salt

Addito salis grano
With a grain of salt added
    –Pliny the Elder 23.149, describing a recipe for making an antidote to poison.

🏛 Tell it to the marines. / Talk to the hand.

Apud novercam querere.

Complain to your stepmother.

> —Plautus, *Pseud.* 314.

🏛 The facts speak for themselves.

τὸ πρᾶγμα φανερόν ἐστιν, αὐτὸ γὰρ βοᾷ.

The matter is clear, he proclaims it.

> —Aristophanes, *Vesp.* 921. A dog put on trial for stealing cheese has just burped in the juryman's face.

τὰ πεπραγμέν᾽ αὐτὰ βοᾷ.

The events proclaim themselves.

> —Demosthenes, *De fals.* 81.

🏛 The long arm of the law

An nescis longas regibus esse manus?

Don't you know that the arms of kings are long?

> —Ovid, *Her.* 17.166.

🏛 The whole is the sum of its parts.

Ex pede Herculem

Hercules, from his foot

> —Plutarch, quoted in Aulus Gellius 1.1.1–3. Proverbial, adapted from the account in a lost work of Plutarch relating how Pythagoras determined

268 • **They Said It First**

Hercules's height by using the
six hundred-foot-long stadium at
Olympia, said to have been paced off
by Hercules.

🏛 There's many a slip between cup and lip.

πολλὰ μεταξὺ πέλει κύλικος, καὶ χείλεος ἄκρου.

There are many things that lie between the cup and the edge of your lip.

> –Palladas, *Greek Anthology* 10.32 (=
> Aulus Gellius 13.18.3).

Nec semper feriet quodcunque minabitur arcus.

The best bow will not always hit something.

> –Horace, *Ars P.* 350.

Inter os atque offam multa intervenire possunt.

Many things can come between mouth and morsel.

> –Cato the Elder, in a speech quoted in
> Aulus Gellius 13.18.1.

🏛 Tiger by the tail

Auribus teneo lupum.

I've got a wolf by the ears.

> –Terence, *Phorm.* 506.

🏛 Time will tell.

Quidquid sub terra est, in apricum proferet aetas / defodiet condetque nitentia.

Whatever is under the earth, time will drag out into the sunlight, just as it will bury and cover up all that shines.

–Horace, *Epist.* 1.6.24–25.

🏛 Timing is everything.

καιρὸν γνῶθι.

Know the right moment.

–Pittachus, cited in Diogenes Laertius 1.4.79.

🏛 To be of two minds

οὐκ οἶδ' ὅττι θέω· δίχα μοι τὰ νοήμματα.

I don't know what I should do; I'm of two minds.

–Sappho, frag. 51.

🏛 To err is human.

Cuiusvis hominis est errare, nullius nisi insipientis in errore perseverare.

It is in any man to err, but it's the sign of a fool alone to persist in error.

–Cicero, *Phil.* 12.5.

τὸ γὰρ ἁμαρτάνειν, ἀνθρώπους ὄντας,
οὐδὲν, οἴμαι, θαυμαστόν.

*To make a mistake, seeing that we are human, is not, I
think, that remarkable.*

–Xenophon, *Cyr.* 5.4.19.

🏛 Too big for one's britches

μηδὲ ὑπὲρ τὸν πόδα ἔστω τὸ ὑπόδημα.

Don't let the sandal be bigger than the foot.

–Lucian, *Pro Im.* 10.

🏛 Too many cooks spoil the broth.

πολλοὶ στρατηγοὶ Καρίαν ἀπώλεσαν.

Too many generals lost Caria.

–Proverb, preserved in Erasmus, *Adages*
4.1607 (= frag. 556, *CAF*).

🏛 Use it or lose it.

**Aera nitent usu; vestis bona quaerit
haberi; canescunt turpi tecta relicta
situ.**

*Brass shines with use; good clothes want to be worn;
abandoned houses age amid foul neglect.*

–Ovid, *Am.* 1.8.51

**At memoria minuitur, credo, nisi eam
exerceas.**

Memory diminishes, I feel, unless you use it.

–Cicero, *Sen.* 21.

🏛 Waste not want not.

Perdendi finem nemo nisi egestas facit.
Nothing except poverty sets a limit on waste.
–Publilius Syrus 508.

🏛 Water over the dam (*or* under the bridge)

Sed haec et vetera et a Graecis.
But that is not only ancient history, it's from the Greeks.
–Cicero, *Tusc.* 1.74.

🏛 What goes around comes around.

Multis terribilis, caveto omnes.
If you are going to be terrifying to many, then be afraid of everyone.
–Periander of Corinth, quoted in Ausonius, *App.* 1.26.

🏛 When in Rome, do as the Romans do.

ἐν θηρίοις δὲ καὶ πιθήκοις ὄντα δεῖ εἶναι πίθηκον.
If you find yourself among beasts and monkeys, then you have to be a monkey.
–Apollodorus, *Adelphoi* frag. 1.3–4 (CAF).

🏛 Where there's smoke there's fire.

> ### Semper tu scito, flamma fumo est proxima.
> *Always know this—fire is the neighbor of smoke.*
> –Plautus, *Curc.* 53.

🏛 Which came first, the chicken or the egg?

> ### Scire ex vobis volo, ovumne prius extiterit an gallina?
> *I want your opinion, did an egg exist first or a chicken?*
> –Macrobius, *Sat.* 6.24.

🏛 You can fool some of the people all of the time, and all of the people some of the time, but you cannot fool all of the people all the time.
(Attributed to P. T. Barnum or Abraham Lincoln.)

> ### Melius omnibus quam singulis creditur: singuli enim decipere et decipi possunt, nemo omnes, neminem omnes fefellerunt.
> *It's better to believe the masses than individuals, for individuals can deceive and be deceived, but no one has ever fooled everybody, nor everyone no one.*
> –Pliny the Younger, *Pan.* 62.9.

🏛 ## You can lead a horse to water, but you can't make it drink.

Stultitia est, pater, venatum ducere invitas canes.

Father, it is foolishness to lead out unwilling dogs to hunt.
–Plautus, *St.* 139.

🏛 ## You can put lipstick on a pig, but it is still a pig.

Non faciunt meliorem equum aurei freni.

Golden bridles don't make the horse better.
–Seneca, *EM* 41.6.

🏛 ## You can't get blood from a turnip.

Aquam a pumice nunc postulas.

Now you are asking for water from pumice stone.
–Plautus, *Per.* 41.

🏛 ## You can't take it with you.

χρήματ' ἔχων οὐδεὶς ἔρχεται εἰς Ἀΐδεω.

No one goes to Hades holding on to his possessions.
–Solon, frag. 24.

🏛 ## You have to walk before you can fly.

Sine pennis volare haud facile est.

It's pretty hard to fly without feathers.
–Plautus, *Poen.* 871.

🏛 **You've got to pay the piper.**

δράσαντι γάρ τοι καὶ παθεῖν ὀφείλεται.

The one doing the deed must also suffer the consequences.
　　　　　　　　–Aeschylus, frag. 655.3 (Mette).

🏛 **You've hit the nail on the head.**

Tetigisti acu.

You've touched it with a needle.
　　　　　　　　–Plautus, *Rud.* 1305.

Appendix A: Pronunciation of Greek

Few things are as daunting as trying to provide a guide on how to pronounce ancient Greek. It is like wearing a target to an archery range. Discussions among classicists over just how to pronounce ancient Greek can approach levels of intensity only matched by discussions of politics around a Thanksgiving table circled by one's relatives. Why?

First, written Greek texts can be read in an unbroken line from the Bronze Age to today's issues of the Athenian newspapers Τα Νέα (*The News*) or Η Βραδυνή (*The Evening Newspaper*), and language pronunciations change over time. For example, while the first newspaper would have been pronounced roughly the same in antiquity as today ("Ta *Nea*"; italics indicate a stressed syllable), an ancient might have pronounced the evening paper as "Hay Bradu*nay*," but the vendor at a kiosk in Athens's Syntagma Square expects to hear "Ee Vrathee*nee*."

Second, little pleases scholars as much as holding heated conversations over issues that mean a great deal to them, but when the bottom line is tallied, are of little value to the average person, such as those for whom this book is written. As a result, the guide that appears here follows an older, traditional set of rules that are out of vogue in some circles, widely used in others, and commonly the source of more heat than illumination. Those interested in the minutiae of the argumentation pro and con need only do an internet search ("ancient Greek pronunciation") to find sites that include recordings. Complaints and quibbles with what follows may be directed to the Department of Lost Causes.

Consonants

B, β	*b*
Γ, γ	*g*; γγ = ng, ἄγγελος = **ang**elos
Δ, δ	*d*
Z, ζ	*ds*, as in "be**ds**"
Θ, θ	*th*
K, κ	*k*
Λ, λ	*l*
M, μ	*m*
N, ν	*n*
Ξ, ξ	*ks* or *x*, as in "a**xe**"
Π, π	*p*
P, ρ	*r*
Σ, σ	*s* (written -ς at the end of a word)
T, τ	*t*
Φ, φ	*ph*
X, χ	*ch* as in "e**ch**o"
Ψ, ψ	*ps*

Vowels and Diphthongs

Elementary Greek students tear their hair out over the vowels. There are only six vowels, but they can be long or short, have a variety of things written above and below them, and are too often in tiny print. Moreover, two vowels can be combined to make diphthongs that produce a single sound, as in the English "field" or "boil." What follows is a simple guide that will enable you to pronounce the Greek satisfactorily.

A, α   *ah,* as in "father"

ᾳ   *ah,* as in "father"

αι   long *i,* as in "light"

αυ   *ou,* as in "**ou**ch"

E, ε   *eh*

ει   long *a* as in "fr**eig**ht"

H, η   *ey* as in "**they**" (transcribed as *ē*)

ῃ   *ey* as in "**they**"

ηυ   rare; if encountered, *ey-oo,* almost like "hey you" without the "h"

I, ι   *i* or *ee;* you will hear even professionals switching

O, o   short *o*

οι   *oy*

ου   *oo*

Υ, υ   *oo*

υι   *oo-ee,* blended together

Ω, ω   long *o, oh* (transcribed as *ō*)

ῳ   long *o, oh*

Wait. It gets worse, because these vowels and diphthongs can be written in a variety of ways.

Breathings: Vowels and diphthongs beginning a word always bear a breathing mark: smooth ἀ ("ah") or rough ἁ ("hah"). Compare αἰ and αἱ. Note that a rough breathing mark routinely appears on the letter Ῥ, ῥ.

Accents: Ancient Greek was a tonal language in that vowels were pronounced at various pitches independent from the stress accent. Unless you know another modern tonal language, it is hard to explain. But try saying these phrases out loud: "Do you **really** believe that?" "Yes, it makes sense." "**Really?**" The stress accent remains on the first syllable, but you'll find yourself changing the pitch on the second "really." There were three pitch marks in ancient Greek. Modern Greek has simplified to one, and it only indicates stress.

The three marks are shown here over an α (ά, ὰ, or ᾶ) and can be combined with breathing marks and with a certain mark *below* the vowel that is shorthand for writing a diphthong with an ι. Thus, you can find things like ᾁ, ᾄ, or ᾳ. For our purposes, treat accents simply as stress marks, ignoring pitch accents and subscripts. So: ἀρχῆς (arch*ēs*; italics indicate stressed syllable) and αὐτῶν (aut*ōn*).

Examples:

μηδὲν ἄγαν	m*ē*den *a*gan
ὁ ὅμοιος τῷ ὁμοίῳ	ho *ho*moios tō ho*moi*ō
οὐκ ἔστιν ἐν πολέμῳ δὶς ἁμαρτεῖν	ouk *es*tin en pol*e*mō dis hamar*tein*
κακὸς δ' αἰδοῖος ἀλήτης	ka*kos* d' ai*doi*os al*ē*tēs

Appendix B: Ancient Authors and People Cited

Far more works from antiquity have been lost to us than have survived. All that is left of the works of many ancient authors are titles and quotations mentioned by other ancient authors whose works do exist and the occasional lines found on papyrus fragments. Such works are called "lost" below. Sometimes we know the name of the work and sometimes only the author's name.

There is no logic to be found behind the accepted conventions for naming ancient authors and their works since they evolved through two millennia of scholarly work. A strict transliteration of Aristotle's name would yield "Aristoteles" and Plato would be "Platon." Various ancient sources even give different names for the same work of literature. For reasons lost in the history of scholarship, the works of a given Greek author are regularly listed in English (Plato's *Republic*), in a Latin translation (Xenophon's *Memorabilia*), or in a transliteration of the Greek (Menander's *Epitrepontes*). Some Latin works are generally known only by their Latin titles, like Cicero's *De Officiis*, while others are translated. There's no accounting for it. It is what it is (another quote, most recently made famous by Bill Belichick, coach of the New England Patriots).

Those who have been initiated into this chaos through study of the classics do not even notice the oddness of our accepted practices, but it can be daunting for the uninitiated. The list that follows, then, seeks to maintain current best practice while offering help for the nonprofessional who might want to pursue a quote, author, or work further. English titles of works tend to follow those given in the Loeb editions. Abbreviations are those generally used by the *Oxford Classical Dictionary* and the major Latin and Greek lexicons.

Notes

1. Only works cited in this book are listed.

2. After the date in each entry, a G (Greek) or L (Latin) indicates the language in which the author wrote.

3. The use of square brackets around a title means that the work is spuriously attributed to that author.

Aelian (ca. 170–ca. 235 CE), G.
Claudius Aelianus was born in Praeneste but learned Greek from a sophistic teacher. His output was quite varied and included polemics and essays, now lost. His remaining works are eclectic and sometimes uncritical, especially when reporting "facts" about animals.
Historical Miscellany (*Varia Historia; VH*)

Aeschylus (525?–456 BCE), G.
Athenian tragedian, forerunner of Sophocles and Euripides. Fought in the Battle of Marathon (490 BCE). Seven of his plays survive.
Agamemnon (*Ag.*)
Prometheus Bound (*PV*)

Aesop (6th century BCE), G.
Known for his animal-based fables, Aesop was said to be a Greek slave. He is mentioned by Herodotus, who places him in the sixth century BCE, but most details of his life were fictions added later. None of his writings survive, but a collection of stories circulated under his name as early as the fifth century BCE. Later authors such as Avianus, Babrius, and Phaedrus carried on the fabulist tradition, often basing their stories on Aesop's. See the works of Chambry and Perry.

Alcaeus (b. ca. 625 BCE), G.
Greek lyric poet from Mytilene on Lesbos. His poetry often deals with the politics of Lesbos and the tyrant Pittacus.

Alcman (fl. mid-to-late 7th century BCE), G.
Greek lyric poet of some renown, although most of his works have been lost. Most of his poems are choral in nature.

(St.) Ambrose (ca. 340–397 CE), L.
Born in Gaul, he became bishop of Milan and the author of many works, including letters, biblical commentaries, and hymns. He was prominent in his opposition against the emperor Theodosius and the heretical doctrine known as Arianism.

Ammianus Marcellinus (ca. 330–395 CE), L.
Although Greek, he sought in his *History* (*Rerum Gestarum Libri*) to pick up the story of Rome where the work of Tacitus ends (96 CE) and to bring it up to Rome's defeat at Adrianople (378 CE).

Amphis (ca. 4th century BCE), G.
Amphis was the author of Greek comedies. His works have not survived, but we have the names of twenty-eight of his plays and fragments of his works quoted by others. Cited here is his *Gynaecocratia* (*Women in Power*).

Anacreon (b. ca. 570 BCE), G.
Anacreon was a Greek lyric poet born in Asia Minor. When his city was threatened by Persia, he moved to Thrace and Samos. He eventually came to Athens. His poems are left to us largely as fragments and deal mostly with love and the pleasures of the banquet. The title *Anacreontea* refers to a collection of Hellenistic poems once erroneously thought to be by Anacreon.

Anaxagoras (ca. 500–428 BCE), G.
The first philosopher to reside in Athens, he was originally from Ionia. He later fled Athens under a charge of "impiety." His one book, now lost, was called *On Nature* and is best remembered for its theory that *Nous* (Mind) was the origin and animating principle of all living things.

Antiphanes (first play, 385 CE), G.
A writer of Greek comedies who probably wrote over three hundred plays. We have the titles of almost half of them, but his work survives only in about 330 citations. Some, however, consist of lengthy excerpts from his work.

Antisthenes (mid-5th–mid-4th c. BCE), G.
Philosopher and acquaintance of Socrates. He wrote voluminously, but all his works are lost.

Apelles (fl. latter part of 4th c. BCE), G.
Born in Colophon, he was generally regarded in antiquity as the best of all painters. Alexander the Great would allow no other painter to paint him.

Apollodorus (3rd c. BCE), G.
Born in Carystus, a town on the island of Euboea, he was a late author of Greek comedy. His work remains to us only in fragments.

Appius Claudius Caecus (censor 312; consul 307 and 296 BCE), L.
Best known for his hand in commissioning the Via Appia and Rome's first aqueduct, he was primarily a Roman politician. He composed *Sententiae* (*Aphorisms*) imitating Pythagoras and is the earliest Roman prose author known to us.

Apuleius (ca. 125–ca. 170 CE), L.
Lucius Apuleius was African by birth. He traveled extensively and wrote many lectures and books, the most famous of which is an early form of the novel and is known under two names—*Metamorphoses* and *The Golden Ass.*
  Apologia (*Apol.*)
  Florida (*Flor.*)

Arcesilaus (316–241 BCE), G.
Greek philosopher who served as head of the Academy from 268 BCE and is often called the founder of the Middle Academy. His works are lost, but his influence was strong on those who followed.

Archias (d. 379 BCE), G.
Theban official who drunkenly ignored a letter spelling out a pending attack by exiles. This cost him his life.

Aristophanes (ca. 445–ca. 385 BCE), G.
Athenian author of eleven surviving comedies from the fifth and early fourth centuries. Aristophanes was known for his bawdy humor, commentary on current events, and inventive plots.
> *Birds* (*Av.*)
> *Clouds* (*Nub.*)
> *Peace* (*Pax*)
> *Wasps* (*Vesp.*)

Aristotle (384–322 BCE), G.
A pupil of Plato, he too became a prolific author. His works cover philosophy, ethics, and natural history, to name a few. Philip II of Macedon engaged Aristotle to tutor the young Alexander the Great.
> *Great Ethics* (*Mag. Mor.*)
> *Metaphysics* (*Metaph.*)
> *Nicomachean Ethics* (*Eth. Nic.*)
> *Physics* (*Ph.*)
> *Politics* (*Pol.*)

(St.) Athanasius (ca. 296–373 CE), G.
Born in Alexandria, he became a major theologian and defender of Christian orthodoxy, especially against Arianism. His *Life of Antony* concerns the Egyptian ascetic Antony the Great (251–356 CE).

Athenaeus (fl. ca. 200 CE), G.
Probably from Naucratis, Egypt, he wrote a very long work, of which fifteen books survive. The title, *Deipnosophistae* (*Learned Ones at Dinner*), tells its format, in which scholars have a days-long, wide-ranging discussion. In the process, they quote about 1,250 ancient authors.

Athenodorus (1st c. BCE–?), G.
Born in Cilicia, he came to Rome with Octavian to serve as court philosopher, in which role he taught the young Claudius.

Attalus (fl. early 1st c. CE), G.
The Stoic philosopher who was the teacher of Seneca the Younger.

(St.) Augustine of Hippo (354–430 CE), L.
Born in Thagaste (modern Algeria), Augustine began a career in rhetoric. He soon turned to philosophy and ultimately converted to Christianity, becoming bishop of Hippo Regius in northern Africa. His numerous theological and philosophical writings also include letters.
  Letters (*Epistulae; Ep.*)

Augustus (63 BCE–14 CE), L.
Born Gaius Octavius and known in history books as Octavian, he emerged as the first Roman emperor following the civil wars that wracked Rome, eventually taking on the name Augustus, "revered."

Aulus Gellius (ca. 130–180 CE), L.
Aulus Gellius is the author of a collection of random jottings called *Atticae Noctes* (*Attic Nights*). The work is in twenty books and consists of short essays on a wide variety of subjects arising from his studies when he lived in Attica, the deme that included Athens.

Aurelius, Marcus (121–180 CE), G.
Of Spanish heritage, he became a favorite at the courts of the emperor Hadrian, and he himself served as emperor from 161 to 180 CE. A devout Stoic, his *Meditations* were self-reflections on Stoicism written down throughout his life.

Ausonius (310–ca. 393 CE), L.
Decimus Magnus Ausonius was born in what today is Bordeaux, France. He wrote prodigiously. His most famous poems deal with a poetic description of his life and of the Moselle River.
  Appendix of Ausonius (*App.*)
  Epigrams (*Epig.*)
  Technopaegnion (*Technop.*)

Avianus (fl. ca. 400 CE), L.
Latin author of forty-two fables in the Aesopic tradition, often using Babrius as a source.

Babrius (unsure dates), G.
Valerius (?) Babrius is a little known author of fables in the Aesopic tradition. His work was largely forgotten until a manuscript containing 123 of his fables was discovered at the convent of St. Laura on Mount Athos.

Bias of Priene (before mid-6th c. BCE), G.
Bias was a legendary character for the Greeks, being considered one of their Seven Sages. Best known as an advocate, he also wrote poetry. We have none of his writings, but he is often quoted by later authors.

Bion (ca. 335–245 BCE), G.
The son of a freedman and a prostitute, Bion was born near the Black Sea; his entire family was sold as slaves. He eventually made his way to Rome, where he studied philosophy. Some in antiquity depicted him as of dubious moral character and none of his works survive. See his biography in Diogenes Laertius 4.7.

Brutus (ca. 85–42 BCE), L.
Marcus Junius Brutus was a prominent participant in the turbulent politics of the later first century BCE. Brutus, along with Cassius, played a prominent role in the assassination of Julius Caesar.

Caecilius Statius (d. 168 BCE), L.
Roman writer of comedies who was born in Gaul. Only titles and about 280 lines survive.

Caesar (100–44 BCE), L.
Gaius Julius Caesar was a Roman general and dictator. Caesar first rose to prominence in successful military campaigns against the Gauls. Amid the turmoil that marked the end of the period of the Republic in Rome, he rose to the top in a civil war against rivals like Pompey the Great, which he also chronicled. He was assassinated on March 15, 44 BCE by opponents who feared he was destroying Rome's traditional rule as a republic.

    Civil War (Bellum Civile; B Civ.)
    Gallic War (Bellum Gallicum; B Gall.)

Calgacus (fl. 1st c. CE), Celtic.
Chieftain from Caledonia (Scotland) who opposed the Roman invasion as described by Tacitus.

Callimachus (fl. late 3rd c. BCE), G.
A Greek poet and scholar, he was also head of the Library at Alexandria. He flourished under Ptolemy II, who commissioned him to catalog all the books in the Library. His poetry ranges from epigrams to hymns and is often cryptic, laden with literary references.

Cassius (before 85–42 BCE), L.
Gaius Cassius Longinus was a prominent Roman politician and soldier, best known for his participation in the assassination of Julius Caesar. He was husband to Junia Tertia, the half-sister of Brutus.

Cato the Elder (234–149 BCE), L.
Marcus Porcius Cato was a censor and prolific author, although only his work on agriculture has come to us intact. Most quotes given under the name Cato in this book actually refer to a late classical (3rd c. CE?) collection of sayings (*Disticha Catonis*) that went on to become an important textbook during the Middle Ages. There are many versions of this work, and the name of the author is often given as Dionysius Cato.
> *Distichs of Cato (Disticha Catonis; Dist.)*
> *On Agriculture (De Agricultura; Agr.)*

Cato the Younger (95–46 BCE), L.
Marcus Porcius Cato was the great-grandson of Cato the Elder. Born in Utica, he was a major figure in the first century BCE turmoil that culminated in the assassination of Julius Caesar.

Catullus (ca. 84–ca. 54 BCE), L.
Gaius Valerius Catullus was a Roman poet from northern Italy, a contemporary of Caesar, and best known for the poems describing his love affair with Lesbia (a pseudonym for a highborn married woman).

Chabrias (ca. 420–357 BCE), G.
Chabrias was a professional soldier from Athens, serving as general for Athens thirteen times.

Chaeremon (mid-4th c. BCE?), G.
Famed Athenian (?) tragedian, Chaeremon was mildly praised by Aristotle.

Chilon (mid-6th c. BCE), G.
A Spartan philosopher and lyric poet who was listed as one of the Seven Sages of Greece and to whom Diogenes Laertius devotes an entire chapter (1.3).

Cicero (106–43 BCE), L.
Marcus Tullius Cicero was a Roman orator and statesman. He was actively involved in the turmoil that ended the Roman Republic, paying for his involvement with his life. He was a prolific writer and in addition to his speeches, produced works on philosophy, divination, and rhetoric, as well as a vast collection of letters.

    Academics (*Academica; Acad.*)
    Brutus (*Brut.*)
    Classification of Oratory (*Partitiones Oratoriae; Part.*)
    In Defense of Archias (*Pro Archia; Arch.*)
    In Defense of Flaccus (*Pro Flacco; Flac.*)
    In Defense of Milo (*Pro Milone; Mil.*)
    In Defense of Plancius (*Pro Plancio; Planc.*)
    In Defense of Tullius (*Pro Tullio; Tul.*)
    Letters to Atticus (*Att.*)
    Letters to Friends (*Fam.*)
    Letters to Quintus (*Q. fr.*)
    On Boundaries (*De Finibus; Fin.*)
    On Divination (*De Divinatione; Div.*)
    On Duties (*De Officiis; Off.*)
    On Friendship (*De Amicitia; Amic.*)
    On Laws (*De Legibus; Leg.*)
    On Old Age (*De Senectute; Sen.*)

On Rhetorical Invention (De Inventione Rhetorica; Inv. rhet.)
On the Nature of the Gods (De Natura Deorum; N.D.)
On the Orator (De Oratore; De Orat.)
On the Republic (De Re Publica; Rep.)
Orator (Orat.)
Philippics (Phil.)
[Rhetoric, for Herrenius (Rhetorica ad Herrenium; Her.)]
Tusculan Disputations (Tusc.)
Verrine Orations (Verr.)

Claudian (4th or 5th c. CE), L.
Though Greek by birth, Claudius Claudianus was one of the last great Latin poets who wrote in the classical tradition.
Against Rufinus (In Rufinum; In Ruf.)
Panegyric on the Consulship of Manlius Theodorus (De Consulatu Manlii Theodori)
Rape of Persephone (De Raptu Proserpinae)

Cleobulus (fl. mid-6th c. BCE), G.
One of the Greek Seven Sages, he was from Lindos on the island of Rhodes and wrote poetry, of which only fragments remain.

Curtius, Quintus (1st or early 2nd c. CE), L.
Quintus Curtius Rufus probably wrote during the reign of Claudius, and his main work is a history of Alexander the Great, especially valuable for its reliance on earlier works on Alexander, now lost.

Demetrius of Phaleron (b. ca. 350 BCE), G.
Born in a suburb of Athens, he was involved in politics and was an excellent orator. He also wrote prolifically, but only fragments remain.

Democritus (460–ca. 357 BCE), G.
From Abdera, Thrace, he was a Greek philosopher who, with Leucippus, was a founder of the Greek version of atomic theory. He wrote many works, but only fragments remain. He is frequently referred to and depicted as the "laughing" philosopher since he saw the humor in the human condition.

Demosthenes (384–322 BCE), G.
Athenian orator and speech writer who became famous for his opposition to the threatened takeover of Greece by Philip II of Macedon, the father of Alexander the Great. Sixty-one speeches have come down to us under his name, although some are undoubtedly spuriously attributed.
    On the False Embassy (De fals.)

Diogenes Laertius (early 3rd c. BCE?), G.
Nothing is known about his life. His only surviving work, *Lives of the Eminent Philosophers,* traces chronologically the Greek philosophers from Thales to Epicurus, giving brief biographies, lists of works, and favorite sayings of each.

Diogenes of Sinope (ca. 410–ca. 321 BCE), G.
Exiled from Sinope (in modern Turkey, along the Black Sea) and charged with a fiscal crime against the state, he spent the rest of his life in exile, mostly at Athens. Founder of the Cynic school of philosophy, he lived his life "naturally," often engaging in typically private bodily functions in full view of passers-by.

Diogenianus (fl. reign of Hadrian, 117–138 CE), G.
Greek grammarian from the eastern empire, famous for a collection of aphorisms taken from poetical works. His work is an abridgement of earlier works. A list of proverbs under his name exists and is preserved in *Paroemiographi Graeci* (Gaisford, 1836, 155–227), available online through Hathi Trust (www.hathitrust.org). See also *Corpus Paroemiographorum Graecorum* (von Leutsch and Schneidewin 1839).

Dionysius Cato. See **Cato the Elder.**

Dionysius of Halicarnassus (fl. 30 BCE and after), G.
Moved to Rome during Augustus's reign, where he became a well-known rhetorician, literary critic and historian. His history treated Rome from its mythological beginnings to the start of the First Punic War.
    [*Art of Rhetoric (Ars Rhetorica; Rhet.)*]

Donatus (4th c. CE), L.
Aelius Donatus was a Latin grammarian and the teacher of St. Jerome. He also wrote commentaries on the plays of Terence and on Vergil.

Ennius (239–169 BCE), L.
Born in Calabria, Quintus Ennius was eventually taken to Rome by Cato the Elder. He is known for his tragedies and *Annals*, an epic poem relating the history of Rome. Unfortunately, only fragments of his works remain.

Epicharmus (late 6th?–early 5th c. BCE), G.
A writer of comedies who worked, not at Athens, but in Sicily, at the court of Hieron of Syracuse. None of his plays survive. K-A list him under the Doric authors.

Epictetus (ca. 50–120 CE), G.
Born a slave and once owned by Nero's secretary, Epictetus was a Stoic philosopher. His work influenced that of Marcus Aurelius. The historian Arrian attended his lectures and later published his notes in two works.
>   *Discourses*
>   *Handbook* (*Encheiridion; Ench.*)

Epicurus (341–271 BCE), G.
Greek philosopher, born on Samos, but relocated to Athens where he established the philosophical school that bears his name. Building on the work of Democritus, he believed that all things were made up of atoms ("indivisible things") and preached a life centered on peace of mind.

Erasmus (1466–1536 CE), L.
One of the foremost scholars of his day, the Dutch priest Desiderius Erasmus of Rotterdam wrote extensively on many subjects. He is relevant here because of his *Adagia*, an extensive collection of quotations and sayings in Latin and Greek, gleaned from his wide reading of classical authors.
>   *Adages* (*Adagia*; sometimes called the *Chiliades*)

Euripides (ca. 485–406 BCE), G.
Greek tragedian who followed Aeschylus and was a contemporary of Sophocles. More of his plays survive than of either Aeschylus or Sophocles, but he won first prize only five times. His portrayal of downtrodden characters was often parodied by Aristophanes.

> *Alcestis (Alc.)*
> *Hecuba (Hec.)*
> *Heraclidae (Heracl.)*
> *Hippolytus (Hipp.)*
> *Ion*
> *Medea (Med.)*
> *Phoenician Women (Phoen.)*
> *Rhesus (Rhes.)*
> *Suppliant Women (Supp.)*
> *Thesmophoriazousae (Thesm.)*

Florus (b. ca. 74 CE), L.
Publius Annius Florus was a poet and friend of the emperor Hadrian. His poems and fragments are most readily found in volume 2 of the Loeb edition of *Minor Latin Poets* (Duff and Duff, 1961).

> *On the Quality of Life (De Qualitate Vitae)*

Hadrian (76–138 CE), L.
Publius Aelius Hadrianus was born in Spain but later became a favorite of Trajan, upon whose death he became emperor and ruled from 117 until his death.

Heraclitus (fl. ca. 500 BCE) G.
Early philosopher from Ephesus who believed things are in constant flux.

Herodotus (ca. 490–ca. 425 BCE), G.
Born in Halicarnassus into a well-known family, he fell victim to local politics and went into exile on Samos. He then traveled widely, eventually coming to Athens, where he became friends with Pericles. His history of the Persian Wars earned him the title "father of history."

Hesiod (fl. ca. 700 BCE), G.

Born in Boeotia, Hesiod is one of the oldest known Greek poets, and wrote two didactic poems in the same epic meter Homer used for his poems. The *Theogony* traces the origin of the gods. The *Works and Days* is directed to his brother and offers advice on how best to run one's life.

> *Works and Days* (*Opera et Dies; Op.*)

Hippocrates (fl. 5th c. BCE), G.

A famous physician from the island of Cos, under whose name many works survive, though scholars doubt some of the attributions. Important here for the collection of aphorisms that appeared under his name.

Hippolytus (ca. 170–ca. 236 CE), G.

Roman theologian and martyr. After falling out with the Roman papacy, he returned to the church and became a prolific apologist and defender of the faith.

> *Refutation of All Heresies* (*Refutatio Omnium Haeresium; Haer.*)

Homer (8th c. BCE?), G.

Nothing factual is known of Homer's life. The oldest extant Greek poet, known for his *Iliad* and *Odyssey*, was believed to have been a single, real person throughout antiquity, but modern scholarship often puts more stress on the idea of his poems originating as the product of a tradition of oral epic poetry.

> *Iliad* (*Il.*)
> *Odyssey* (*Od.*)

Horace (65–8 BCE), L.

Quintus Horatius Flaccus was a favored poet under the reign of Augustus. Born in Venusia in southern Italy and educated in Greece, he joined the army of Brutus against the future Augustus. Nevertheless, his poetry soon made him a favorite at court, along with the likes of Vergil and Propertius.

The Art of Poetry (Ars Poetica; Ars. P.)
Odes (Carmina; Carm.)
Epistles (Epist.)
Satires (Sat.)

Isocrates (436–338 BCE), G.
Athenian orator, author, and teacher whose writings helped shape the politics of his time. His speeches were not delivered by him in person, but served more as political opinion pieces.
To Demonicus (Dem.)
To Nicocles (Nic.)

(St.) Jerome (ca. 347–420 CE), L.
Born Eusebius Sophronius Hieronymus in Stridon, Dalmatia, he became a priest. He wrote hagiography, theology, history, commentaries, letters, and, most famously, translated the Bible from the original into Latin, producing the Vulgate Bible.
Decree of Master Gratian (Decretum Magistri Gratiani;
Decr. Gr.)
Letters (Epistulae; Ep.)

Junia Tertia (ca. 75 BCE–22 CE), L.
Half-sister to Marcus Junius Brutus and wife of Gaius Cassius Longinus. She survived the turmoil of the times, dying during the reign of Tiberius, whom she pointedly left out of her will.

Juvenal (fl. early 2nd c. CE), L.
Decimus Junius Juvenalis was born near Rome but little is known of his life, which overlapped that of Martial. His sixteen satires are a dour and pessimistic view of life in Rome under the early emperors.

Laberius (ca. 105–42 BCE), L.
Apparently born in Italy, Decimus Laberius became an author of mimes, a profession below his equestrian rank, and attained some status at it. At his triumphal games, Caesar commanded a contest between Laberius and Publilius Syrus. Publilius won, but Caesar restored equestrian status to Laberius. Only fragments of his work remain.

Livy (59 BCE–17 CE), L.
Titus Livius is the most famous historian of the Augustan Age. Born in northern Italy, he soon moved to Rome and joined Augustus's circle. His massive history of Rome, generally called *Ab Urbe Condita* (*From the City's Founding*), covered the period from the founding of Rome until 9 BCE, and contained 142 books, of which only 1–10 and 21–45 survive.

Lucan (29–65 CE), L.
Like his grandfather, Seneca the Elder, and his uncle, Seneca the Younger, he was born in Spain. Educated in Rome and Athens, he became a familiar of the emperor Nero. His epic poem, *Pharsalia*, treats the civil war between Julius Caesar and Pompey the Great. After falling out with Nero, he joined a conspiracy against him and, along with his uncle, was forced to commit suicide.

Lucian (ca. 120–after 180 CE), G.
Born at Samosata in eastern Turkey, Lucian authored a large number of essays, dialogues, and pure fiction. His *True Story* is a tall tale of wandering, which even takes the main characters to the moon, which is inhabited; *The Dream* follows the adventures of a man who becomes a donkey.

> *Apology for the "Salaried Posts in Great Houses"* (*Apol.*)
> *Against an Ignorant Book Collector* (*Adversus Indoctum et Libros Multos Ementem; Ind.*)
> *Dialogues of the Dead* (*Dialogi mortuorum; Dial. mort.*)
> *Downward Journey* (*Cataplus; Catapl.*)
> *The Dream* (*Somnium; Somn.*)
> *Essays in Portraiture Defended* (*Pro Imaginibus; Pro im.*)
> *The Fly*
> *Hermotimus* (*Herm.*)
> *How to Write History* (*Hist. conscr.*)
> *Timon* (*Tim.*)

Lucretius (98–ca. 55 BCE), L.
Little is known of the life of Titus Lucretius Carus. His six-book poem, *De Rerum Natura* (*On the Nature of Things*), is a didactic epic designed to teach the precepts of Epicurus.

Macrobius (fl. ca. 400 CE), L.
Ambrosius Theodosius Macrobius, a philosopher and author, was probably born in Africa; little else is known of his life. His best-known work is a dialogue held at a banquet during the festival of the Saturnalia.
     Saturnalia (*Sat.*)

Marius, Gaius (157–86 BCE), L.
Famous Roman general who also served as consul seven times. Best remembered for his reform of the Roman army and his armed conflict against Sulla for sole control of Rome and its empire.

Martial (ca. 40–ca. 103 CE), L.
Marcus Valerius Martialis was a native of Spain who moved to Rome in 64 CE. A professional poet, he wrote short poems satirizing individuals and elucidating Roman life and times under the early emperors. Although friends with Seneca the Younger and Lucan, he was not involved in their plots against Nero. Thirteen books of his poetry survive.
     Epigrams (*Epig.*)

Maximus of Tyre (fl. 2nd c. CE), G.
Author of forty-one lectures, delivered in Rome, on a wide variety of philosophical and ethical themes.

Menander (344?–292 BCE), G.
An Athenian, Menander was the leading author of what is called New Comedy (Aristophanes being an author of Old and Middle Comedy). We know the names of over one hundred of his plays, but most were lost. Various excavated papyri, however, have given us one almost complete play and significant fragments of others. His plays were

imitated by the Roman authors Plautus and Terence. The *Monostichoi* is a collection of aphorisms compiled in antiquity from his works. The numbering for the *Monostichoi* used here is that of Jäkel.

> *One-Liners (Monostichoi; Mon.)*

Nepos, Cornelius (ca. 110–24 BCE, L).
From northern Italy, he moved to Rome, where he knew Cicero and Catullus. The first known Latin biographer.

> *Thrasybulus (Thr.)*

Nicostratus (uncertain dates), G.
Two ancient Greek writers of comedy bore this name. One, it was claimed, was the son of Aristophanes and wrote Middle Comedy. The other, later poet wrote New Comedy. No whole works survive of either.

Nonius (early 4th c. CE?), L.
Nonius Marcellus wrote a twenty-volume encyclopedia/dictionary on grammar and usage containing quotes from Republican era authors. In so doing, he preserved pieces of now lost works.

Numidicus (late 3rd–early 2nd c. BCE), L.
Quintus Caecilius Metellus Numidicus was a Roman politician who became censor in 102 BCE.

Ovid (43 BCE–17 CE), L.
Born in Sulmo, in the Abruzzo area of Italy, Publius Ovidius Naso soon moved to Rome, where he became a renowned poet in the time of Augustus. His early works dealt with love, and he is best known today for his *Metamorphoses*. However due, as he says, "to a poem and an error" he was exiled to a remote part of the Black Sea. Even here he produced remarkable poetry.

> *Art of Love (Ars Amatoria; Ars)*
> *Letters from Heroines (Heroides; Her.)*
> *Letters from Pontus (Epistulae ex Ponto; Pont.)*
> *Loves (Amores; Am.)*
> *Metamorphoses (Met.)*

On the Roman Calendar (Fasti; Fast.)
Remedies for Love (Remedia Amoris; Rem.)
Sorrows (Tristia; Tr.)

Palladas (4th c. BCE), G.
From Alexandria, Egypt, known only from his 150+ poems preserved in the *Greek Anthology.*

Pausanias (fl. ca. 150 CE), G.
Born in Roman-ruled Lydia, Pausanias composed a lengthy travelogue of Greece, noting its monuments in great detail and providing valuable information on treasures since lost.

Periander of Corinth (ruled 627–587 BCE), G.
Served as tyrant of Corinth and became the archetype of a ruthless tyrant.

Persius (34–62 CE), L.
Aulus Persius Flaccus was an Etruscan-born satirist who wrote his *Satires* during the reign of Nero.

Petronius (1st c. CE), L.
This is the name associated with the long satirical work entitled *Satyrica,* of which we have fragments. Some claim he was the Petronius who was named *arbiter elegentiae*, "fashion master," to the court of Nero, but was forced to commit suicide in 66 CE. The identification, however, is unsure.

Phaedrus (ca. 15 BCE–50 CE), L.
Gaius Julius Phaedrus was a slave from northwest Greece. He received his freedom from Augustus and wrote five books of fables in the tradition of Aesop.

Philemon (365?–265 BCE), G.
A Syracusan comic poet (New Comedy) who wrote almost one hundred comedies and was granted Athenian citizenship. Only fragments remain.

Philetas (b. ca. 340 BCE), G.
Poet and scholar from the island of Cos. Tutor of king Ptolemy II Philadelphus, Macedonian ruler of Egypt.

Philonides (fl. 450–410 BCE), G.
Athenian comic poet, also known for producing plays of Aristophanes.

Philostratus the Elder (b. ca. 190 CE), G.
From Lemnos, Philostratus is known for his work in the genre called *ekphrasis,* which deals with describing works of art in words. His *Eikones,* or *Imagines,* contains descriptions of sixty-five paintings. He is to be differentiated from another Philostratus, probably his grandson, who wrote seventeen similar descriptions.
    Letters (Epistulae; Ep.)

Phocylides (early 6th c. BCE), G.
This is the name given to the author of poems concerned with wise sayings (so-called gnomic poetry). A few poems and fragments survive. A set of *sententiae,* or aphorisms, was created under Phocylides's name at a much later date and is referred to as Pseudo-Phocylides.

Pinarius Rusca, Marcus (late 2nd c. BCE), L.
Marcus Pinarius Rusca was a member of a prominent Roman family best known for proposing a bill in 180 BCE that established the minimum age for holding various offices in the Roman government.

Pindar (ca. 518–438 BCE), G.
A native of Boeotia, he became famous as a lyric poet who produced a variety of types of poetry. He is best known for the odes he composed for victors at the four great Panhellenic athletic competitions in Greece
    Nemean Odes (Nem.)

Pittachus (ca. 650–570 BCE), G.
Statesman, lawgiver, and ruler of Mytilene on Lesbos.

Plato (427–347 BCE), G.

An Athenian of noble birth, Plato began by writing poetry, but upon meeting Socrates, devoted his life to philosophy. After his teacher's death, he traveled widely and even tutored a tyrant of Sicily. Returning to Athens, he founded a philosophical school, the Academy. His writings are prodigious, the best known being his Socratic dialogues and the *Republic*.

> *Cratylus* (*Cra.*)
> *Gorgias* (*Grg.*)
> *Laws* (*Leg.*)
> *Republic* (*Resp.*)
> *Theaetetus* (*Tht.*)

Plautus (ca. 250–184 BCE), L.

Titus Macc(i)us Plautus was a writer of some 130 comedies, twenty of which survive intact. He, like Terence, adapted Greek plays from New Comedy authors like Menander and presented them as *fabulae palliatae*, "plays in Greek dress." He was quite popular in his day, and his influence is seen in the works of Shakespeare and Molière.

> *Amphitryon* (*Amph.*)
> *The Braggart Soldier* (*Miles Gloriosus; Mil.*)
> *The Captives* (*Captivi; Capt.*)
> *Casina* (*Cas.*)
> *Comedy of Asses* (*Asinaria; Asin.*)
> *Curculio* (*Curc.*)
> *Epidicus* (*Epid.*)
> *The Ghost* (*Mostellaria; Mostell.*)
> *The Little Carthaginian* (*Poenulus; Poen.*)
> *The Merchant* (*Mercator; Merc.*)
> *The Persian* (*Persa; Per.*)
> *The Pot of Gold* (*Aulularia; Aul.*)
> *Pseudolus* (*Pseud.*)
> *The Rope* (*Rudens; Rud.*)

Stichus (St.)
Three-Dollar Day (Trinummus; Trin.)
The Two Bacchises (Bacch.)

Pliny the Elder (23–79 CE), L.
Gaius Plinius Secundus was born in northern Italy near the Alps. He began his career in the army and held governmental jobs, all while writing prolifically. His remaining work, the *Naturalis Historia (Natural History)*, was a vast (ten Loeb volumes) encyclopedia covering every aspect of the world around him. Pliny died in the eruption of Mt. Vesuvius when he went toward the volcano to study it.

Pliny the Younger (ca. 61–112 CE), L.
Gaius Plinius Caecilius Secundus was born in northern Italy and was raised by his uncle, Pliny the Elder. He practiced law and held governmental positions, the best known of which was governor of Bithynia-Pontus. We have 247 of his letters; especially notable are those to Trajan and Tacitus, among which are references to Christians and a description of the eruption of Mt. Vesuvius in 79 CE.
> *Letters (Epistulae; Ep.)*
> *Panegyricus (Pan.)*

Plutarch (before 50–after 120 CE), G.
His Roman name, Lucius Mestrius Plutarchus, reminds us that Plutarch was a Roman citizen. He was an incredibly prolific author, known especially for biography, philosophy, and essays. The titles of his *Lives* are cited simply by the name of their subject (e.g., *Julius Caesar*). The *Moralia* is a collection of essays, each with its own title.
> *Moralia*
> > *Advice to Bride and Groom (Coniugalia Praecepta; Coniug.)*
> > *On Compliancy (Vit. pud.)*
> > *On Exile (De exil.)*
> > *On the Delays of the Divine Vengeance (De Sera Numinis Vindicta; De sera)*

On the Obsolescence of Oracles (De Defectu
  Oraculorum; De def. or.)
Sayings of Kings and Commanders (Regum et
  Imperatorum Apophthegmata; Apoph. bas.)
Sayings of Romans (Apophthegmata Romana;
  Apoph. Rom.)
Symposiacs (Symp.)
Table Talk (Quaestiones convivales; Q Conv.)
Whether an Old Man Should Engage in Public Affairs
  (An Seni Respublica Gerenda Sit; An seni.)
Lives
  Julius Caesar (Caes.)
  Pelopidas (Pel.)
  Pericles (Per.)
  Pompey (Pomp.)
  Solon (Sol.)

Praxilla (fl. 451 BCE), G.
Born in Sicyon, she was a lyric poet who wrote hymns, dithyrambs, and drinking songs. She was so well regarded in antiquity that the famous sculptor Lysippus produced a sculpture of her. Only a few fragments of her work survive.

Propertius (ca. 50 BCE–after 16 CE), L.
Born in what is modern Assisi, Sextus Propertius moved to Rome, where he became one of the premier poets in the circle of Maecenas. We have four books of his elegies, many of which center around his love for a certain Cynthia.

Protagoras (ca. 490–420 BCE), G.
Born in Abdera, Thrace, he is one of the earliest and best-known sophists (itinerant philosophers/rhetoricians). He traveled throughout the Greek world. His works are lost, but he is portrayed in Plato's dialogue named after him.

Publilius Syrus (1st c. BCE), L.
A slave brought to Rome from Syria, Publilius was freed by his master, who appreciated his wit. Publilius went on to be a successful author of mimes (see **Laberius**). All that is left of his work is an alphabetical list of notable aphorisms from his plays. Note that editions of his works differ in numbering and content, depending on which manuscript tradition editors choose to trust. Publilius was one of the "quote magnets" referred to in the introduction, and undoubtedly many of the sayings attributed to him were written by someone else.

Pythagoras (b. ca. 550 BCE), G.
Born on Samos, he was an influential early philosopher and mathematician whose works survive only in fragments.

Quintilian (ca. 35–95 CE), L.
Marcus Fabius Quintilianus was a Spaniard by birth, who went on to become a Roman advocate and authority on oratory, which he taught for twenty years. His remaining book, the *Institutio Oratoria* (*Training in Oratory*), traces the proper training for an orator from birth until death.

Sallust (ca. 86–35 BCE), L.
Gaius Sallustius Crispus was a Sabine by birth, born in the area just northwest of Rome. When in government, he became embroiled in the turmoil surrounding Caesar's rise to power. We have his full accounts of the wars with Catiline and Jugurtha, and fragments of his *Histories*.
  [*Letters to Caesar* (*Ad Caes. sen.*)]
  War with Catiline (*Bellum Catilinae; Cat.*)

Sappho (late 7th–6th c. BCE), G.
Greek lyric poet born on Lesbos. She wrote nine books of poetry in a wide variety of meters. Her poems are notable for their vivid revelation of personal feelings. Substantial fragments of two new poems were recently discovered.

Scriptores Historiae Augustae (SHA)
This composite title, often referred to as the *Authors of the Augustan History*, refers to a collection of biographies of the emperors who ruled between 117–284 CE. The names of six different authors are attributed to various lives, which are modeled on those written by Suetonius.

> *Hadrian (Hadr.)*
> *Severus Alexander (Sev.)*
> *Tacitus (Tac.)*

Seneca the Elder (ca. 55 BCE–ca. 40 CE), L.
Born in Córdoba, Spain, Lucius Annaeus Seneca moved to Rome and became a well-known rhetorician. His surviving works consist of model exercises and debates used in the study of oratory. Father of Seneca the Younger.

> *Imaginary Legal Cases (Controversiae; Controv.)*

Seneca (the Younger) (ca. 4 BCE–65 CE), L.
Born in Córdoba, Spain, Lucius Annaeus Seneca was the second son of his older namesake. He was a Stoic philosopher who was equally involved in politics. He served as Nero's tutor, only to be condemned to death for his participation in an aborted conspiracy against him. His most influential works are philosophical essays.

> *Epistles (Epistulae Morales; EM)*
> *Hercules Gone Mad (Hercules Furens; Herc. F.)*
> *Medea (Med.)*
> *Natural Questions (Quaestiones Naturales; Q Nat.)*
> *Octavia (Oct.)*
> *Oedipus (Oed.)*
> *On Anger (De Ira; Ira)*
> *On Benefits (De Beneficiis; Ben.)*
> *On Consolation, to Marcia (De Consolatione ad Marciam;*
>   *Cons. Marc.)*
> *[On Morals (De Moribus; Mor.)]*
> *On Providence (De Providentia; Prov.)*

On the Happy Life (De Vita Beata; Vit.)
On the Shortness of Life (De Brevitate Vitae; Brev. vit)
On Tranquility of Mind (De Tranquilitate Animi; Tranq.)
Phoenician Women (Phoen.)
Pumpkinification of Claudius (Apocolocyntosis; Apoc.)
[*Remedies against the Blows of Fortune (De Remediis*
   Fortuitorum; Rem.)]
Thyestes (Thy.)
Trojan Women (Tro.)

Severus Alexander (ca. 207–35 CE), L.
Roman emperor from 222 to 235 CE.

Sextus Empiricus (fl. 200 CE), G.
Greek physician and philosopher whose surviving works provide the best evidence for the philosophical branch of skepticism known as Pyrrhonism.

Silius Italicus (ca. 26–102 CE), L.
Of unsure birthplace, Silius became a noted orator and politician who retired to Campania and committed suicide in the face of cancer. His remaining work is the *Punica (Punic Wars)*, an epic poem about the Second Punic War and the longest extant poem in Latin.

Simonides (b. ca. 556 BCE), G.
A Greek poet from the island of Ceos, his influence was great in later times, but only fragments of his work remain.

Socrates (469–399 BCE), G.
An Athenian philosopher and teacher, Socrates achieved renown for his indefatigable questioning of all beliefs in search of the truth. He developed a strong following among the Athenian youth and antipathy from others. He wrote no books, but is depicted at length in the works of Plato and Xenophon. He fell afoul of those in power and was found guilty of disbelief in the gods and corrupting youth. He was forced to commit suicide by drinking hemlock.

Solon (ca. 640–after 561 BCE), G.
Athenian statesman and poet. During a period of political upheaval, he was elected to bring fairness and economic reform to the Athenian legal system. He wrote about his reforms in his poetry, of which significant samples remain.

Sophocles (496–406 BCE), G.
Athenian dramatist, author of more than 120 plays. He was very successful, winning at least twenty dramatic festival competitions. Seven plays survive intact, as do many fragments, some from plays whose names we know.
> *Ajax* (*Aj.*)
> *Antigone* (*Ant.*)
> *Electra* (*El.*)
> *Oedipus at Colonus* (*OC*)
> *Oedipus Tyrannus* (*OT*)

Statius (ca. 46–ca. 96 CE), L.
Publius Papinius Statius was born in Naples. He became a poet at a young age and was quite popular, winning poetic competitions under Domitian. His epic called the *Thebaid* told the story of the Seven against Thebes, and he planned an epic on Achilles.
> *Thebaid* (*Theb.*)

Stobaeus (early 5th c. CE), G.
John of Stobi, in Macedonia, compiled a large number of extracts from ancient Greek authors, many of which are lost today. The anthology is known by different names: *Floregium* (Latin) and *Anthologia* (Greek), both meaning "gathering of flowers."

Suda (ca. late 10th c. CE), G.
Also known as *Suidas*, this is the title of a sort of historical encyclopedia or lexicon that is itself based on earlier, similar works. It contains many quotations from ancient works now lost.

Suetonius (ca. 70–ca. 130 CE), L.
Born in Lombardy, Italy, Gaius Suetonius Tranquillus wrote biographies of notable ancients, including lost books on famous grammarians and courtesans. He is known to us for his extant *De Vita Caesarum* (*Lives of the Caesars*), covering the emperors from Julius Caesar to Domitian.

> *Augustus* (*Aug.*)
> *Divine Julius* (*Iul.*)
> *Tiberius* (*Tib.*)
> *Vespasian* (*Vesp.*)

Sulpicia (late 1st c. BCE?–early 1st c. CE?), L.
Sulpicia's six poems, preserved as the third book of the Tibullan corpus, represent the largest collection of Latin poetry written by a woman in antiquity. Her poems, addressed to one Cerinthus, are in the elegiac tradition of Propertius and Tibullus.

Sulpicius (ca. 106–43 BCE), L.
Servius Sulpicius Rufus, Sulpicia's father, was a student and friend of Cicero. A supporter of Pompey, he nonetheless served as proconsul of Achaea for Caesar and was a noted jurist.

Tacitus (1) (ca. 56–ca. 120 CE), L.
Publius (or Gaius) Cornelius Tacitus was born in Gaul; he participated fully in Roman politics and became a chronicler of his time period.

> *Agricola* (*Agr.*)
> *Annals* (*Ann.*)
> *Histories* (*Hist.*)

Tacitus (2) (ruled 275–276 CE), L.
Upon the death of the emperor Aurelian, Marcus Claudius Tacitus was chosen emperor. Elderly upon his elevation, he died the next year, killed by his own troops.

Terence (ca. 190–159 BCE), L.
Publius Terentius Afer, as his last name hints, was of African descent. With those of a slightly older Plautus, his six plays constitute the extant corpus of ancient Roman comedy. Both authors based their plays on Greek originals.

> *The Eunuch* (*Eunuchus; Eun.*)
> *Phormio* (*Phorm.*)
> *The Self-Tormentor* (*Heautontimorumenos; Heaut.*)
> *The Woman of Andros* (*Andria; An.*)

Tertullian (ca. 160–ca. 240 CE), L.
Quintus Septimius Florens Tertullianus was a late antique, early Christian author from the environs of Carthage. He was a prolific author of well-written treatises, several of which deal with martyrdom. The work cited here, *De Fuga in Persecutione* (*On Flight from Persecution*), encourages believers not to flee persecution or pay off persecutors, but rather to rely on God to save them.

Theocritus (early 3rd c. BCE), G.
Born in Syracuse, Sicily, Theocritus invented the genre of pastoral poetry. About forty poems are attributed to him, some spuriously.

> *Idylls* (*Id.*)

Theognis (fl. early 6th c. BCE?), G.
A Greek elegiac poet about whose life little is known. A sizeable number of his poems survive, although many are also ascribed to other poets.

Thrasybulus (1) (7th c. BCE), G.
Tyrant of Miletus, a city on the western coast of Asia Minor. Like many tyrants, he was often under threat from pro-oligarchy and pro-democracy factions alike.

Thrasybulus (2) (d. 388 BCE), G.
Athenian general and statesman who came to prominence in the years following the Peloponnesian War. Banished by the Thirty Tyrants, who were put in charge by Sparta, he fled to Thebes and returned with an opposition army, helping restore democracy.

Thucydides (ca. 460–ca. 399 BCE), G.
Born in Athens, he served as a general in the Peloponnesian War, only to be exiled after a failed campaign. His lengthy history of the Peloponnesian War has come to us incomplete, ending in mid-sentence with the affairs of 411/410 BCE.

Tibullus (ca. 50–19 BCE), L.
Albius Tibullus was a Roman elegiac love poet and a friend of both Horace and Ovid. As with others in his genre, the objects of his love were pseudonymous, called Delia, Nemesis, and Marathus. Of the three books that have come to us under his name, only the first two are his (see **Sulpicia**).

Valerius Maximus (fl. reign of Tiberius, 14–37 CE), L.
More a collector of anecdotes than a true historian, he composed nine books filled with information. The work bears various Latin titles, such as *Factorum ac Dictorum Memorabilium Libri IX* (*Nine Books of Memorable Deeds and Sayings*).

Varro (116–27 BCE), L.
Marcus Terentius Varro was born in Sabine territory, near Rome. He had an active political life, which included siding with Pompey against Caesar, from whom he received a pardon. He resembles a modern academic scholar, with over seventy wide-ranging titles ascribed to him. His *De Re Rustica* (*On Agriculture*) has come to us intact. His study *De Lingua Latina* (*On the Latin Language*) was in twenty-five volumes, of which six survive.
  On Agriculture (*De Re Rustica; Rust.*)

Vegetius (late 4th–early 5th c. CE), L.
Nothing is known of Flavius Renatus Vegetius beyond his two surviving works, a handbook on military matters and another handbook on equine veterinary medicine. Though not a soldier himself, Vegetius undertook to summarize earlier military works at the behest of the emperor. The veterinary book was quite influential in the Middle Ages.
  Digest of Military Matters (*Epitoma Rei Militaris; Mil.*)

Vergil (70–19 BCE), L.

The most celebrated Roman poet, Publius Vergilius Maro was born near Mantua, in northern Italy. Three major works survive. *Eclogues* is a collection of ten poems modeled after those of Theocritus. He became a member of the circle of Maecenas and then published the *Georgics*, four books of poetry on the ideal agricultural experience. At the insistence of Augustus, he wrote the *Aeneid*, a twelve-book epic poem tracing the founding of Rome to Aeneas's flight from Troy to Italy.

> *Aeneid* (*Aen.*)
> *Eclogues* (*Ecl.*)

Vespasian (9–79 CE), L.

Titus Flavius Vespasianus was emperor of Rome from 69 to 79 CE. He was known for his quick wit and simple life.

Xenophon (ca. 430–354 BCE), G.

An Athenian by birth, Xenophon enlisted as a mercenary in the Persian army of Cyrus the Younger, who was attempting to unseat Artaxerxes II from the throne. The expedition failed, and Xenophon chronicled the retreat in the *Anabasis*. An author of great range, he also wrote a history that continued that of Thucydides, treatises on hunting and horsemanship, and several Socratic works.

> *Education of Cyrus* (*Cyropaedia; Cyr.*)
> *Household Management* (*Oeconomicus; Oec.*)
> *Remembrances* (*Memorabilia; Mem.*)

Zeno (2nd c. BCE), G.

Born in Sidon in modern Lebanon, he went on to be a famous Epicurean philosopher. None of his works are extant.

Zenodotus (b. 325 BCE), G.

Born in Ephesus, he became the first head of the Library of Alexandria, where he studied epics and lyric poetry.

Bibliography

An asterisk (*) means the source can be found online.

A double asterisk (**) means that earlier editions are available online.

*Bergk, T., ed. *Poetae Lyrici Graeci*. 4th ed. Leipzig: Teubner, 1878–82.

*Chambry, Émile, ed. *Phaedrus:* Fabulae Aesopiae. Paris: Lecoffre, 1900.

Collard, C., and Martin Cropp. *Euripides: Fragments: Oedipus-Chrysippus, Other Fragments*. Cambridge, MA: Harvard University Press, 2008.

*Cramer, J. A., ed. *Anecdota Graeca e Codicibus Manuscriptis Bibliothecae Regiae Parisiensis*. 4 vols. Oxford, 1839. Reprint, Amsterdam: A. M. Hakkert, 1963.

**Diels, Hermann, and Walther Kranz, eds. *Die Fragmente der Vorsokratiker: Griechisch und Deutsch*. 6th ed. 3 vols. Berlin: Weidmann, 1951–52.

Duff, J. W., and A. M. Duff, eds. *Minor Latin Poets*. Cambridge, MA: Harvard University Press, 1961.

Elter, Anton., ed. *Gnomica Homoeomata*. 5 vols. Leipzig: Teubner, 1900.

Freeman, Kathleen, ed., trans. *Ancilla to the Pre-Socratic Philosophers: A Complete Translation of the Fragments in Diels*, Fragmente der Vorsokratiker. Cambridge, MA: Harvard University Press, 1948.

*Gaisford, Thomas, ed. *Paroemiographi Graeci Quorum Pars Nunc Primum ex Codicibus Manuscriptis Vulgatur*. Oxford, 1836.

Jäkel, Siegfried. *Menandri Sententiae*. Leipzig: Teubner, 1964.

Kassel, R., and C. Austin. *Poetae Comici Graeci.* 8 vols. Berlin: De Gruyter, 1983.

*Kock, Theodor. *Comicorum Atticorum Fragmenta.* 3 vols. Leipzig, 1880–88. Reprint, Utrecht: Hes & De Graf, 1976.

Körte, A. and A. Thierfelder. *Menandri Quae Supersunt.* 2nd ed., Leipzig: Teubner, 1959.

Laks, A., G. W. Most, G. Journée, L. Iribarren, and D. Lévystone. *Early Greek Philosophy.* 9 vols. Cambridge, MA: Harvard University Press, 2016. (References given by volume and page.)

*Lindsay, Wallace M., and John Henry Onions, eds. *Nonii Marcelii De Conpendiosa Doctrina Libros XX.* Leipzig: Teubner, 1903.

*Lisdonk, M. L. van Poll-van de, ed. *Opera Omnia Desiderii Erasmi: Ordinis Secundi Tomus Primus.* Leiden, Netherlands: North Holland Imprint, 1993.

*Lyman, Darius, trans. *The Moral Sayings of Publilius Syrus, a Roman Slave: From the Latin.* Cleveland, OH, 1856.

*Meineke, Augustus, ed. *Fragmenta Comicorum Graecorum.* 5 vols. Berlin, 1839–57.

*Meineke, Augustus, ed. *Fragmenta Comicorum Graecorum: Editio Minor.* Berlin, 1847.

*Meineke, Augustus, ed. *Fragmenta Poetarum Comoediae Novae.* Berlin, 1841. Reprint, Berlin: De Gruyter, 1970.

*Meineke, Augustus, ed. *Stobaei Florilegium.* 4 vols. Leipzig, 1856–57.

Mette, H. J. *Die Fragmente der Tragödien des Aischylos.* Berlin: Akademie Verlag, 1959.

*Migne, J.-P., et al., eds. *Patrologiae Cursus Completus: Series Latina.* Paris, 1844–64.

Perry, Ben, ed. *Babrius and Phaedrus.* Cambridge, MA: Harvard University Press, 1965.

*Ribbeck, Otto. *Scaenicae Romanorum Poesis Fragmenta.* Leipzig: Teubner, 1871.

Snell, Bruno, and August Nauck, eds. *Tragicorum Graecorum Fragmenta*. Göttingen, Germany: Vandenhoeck & Ruprecht, 1971.

*Stobaeus. *Ioannis Stobaei Florilegium: Ad Optimorum Librorum Fidem Editum*. Editio stereotypa. Leipzig: Tauchnitz, 1838.

Twain, Mark. *More Maxims of Mark*. Edited by Merle Johnson. New York: privately published, 1927.

Valckenaer, L. C., et al. *Poetae Minores Graeci*. 5 vols. Leipzig, 1823.

*von Leutsch, E. and F. Schneidewin. *Corpus Paroemiographorum Graecorum*. Göttingen, Germany, 1839–51.

*Wachsmuth, Curt, and Otto Hense, eds. *Ioannis Stobaei Anthologium*. Berlin: Weidmann, 1884–1912.

Walther, Hans. *Proverbia Sententiaeque Latinitatis Medii Aevi: Lateinische Sprichwörter und Sentenzen des Mittelalters in Alphabetischer Anordnung*. 6 vols. Göttingen, Germany: Vandenhoeck & Ruprecht, 1963.

Wehrli, F., ed. *Die Schule des Aristoteles*. Basel: Benno Schwabe, 1945–78.

*Werner, Jakob, ed. *Lateinische Sprichwörter und Sinnsprüche des Mittelalters*. Heidelberg: C. Winter, 1912.

*Wölfflin, Eduard, ed. *Publilii Syri Sententiae* [. . .]. Leipzig, 1869.

Index of Authors

Brief identifications are given for modern people. For ancient people see Appendix B, where longer biographies are provided.

Frost, Robert (1874–1963), American poet, multiple Pulitzer Prize winner, 220

Fuller, Thomas (1654–1734), British physician and compiler of proverbs, 39, 153

Gaius Marius, 211, 295

Gandhi, Mahatma (Mohandas Karamchand Gandhi, 1869–1948), Indian civil rights leader and pacifist, 173, 200, 228

Garfield, James A. (1831–81), 20th president of the United States, 100

Gay, John (1685–1732), English poet and dramatist, 73, 241

Gelbart, Larry (1928–2009), American writer for television, screen, and stage, 178

Gemmell, David (1948–2006), British author of historical and fantasy fiction, 133

Getty, Estelle (born Estelle Scher, 1923–2008), American actress best known for television series *The Golden Girls*, 154

Gilbert, W. S. (1836–1911), English dramatist/librettist best known for his collaboration with Arthur Sullivan, 103

Goethe, Johann Wolfgang von (1749–1832), revered German author and polymath, 235

Goldsmith, Oliver (1728–74), Irish playwright, poet, and novelist, 33

Goldstein, Josh (late 19th–early 20th c.), American film producer and writer, 155

Gomez, Vernon Louis "Lefty" (1908–89), American Baseball Hall of Fame pitcher, 136

Goodman, Paul (1911–72), American author and social critic, 207

Gouldman, Graham, 133

Grimm, Jacob (1785–1863) and Wilhelm (1786–1859), German scholars of folktale, 56

Hadrian, 259, 284, 289, 291

Harburg, E. Y. (born Isidore Hochburg, ca. 1897–1981) American lyricist and librettist, 2

Harling, Robert (1951–), American film writer, director, producer, 79

Hazlitt, William (1778–1830), British essayist and literary critic, 102

Heifetz, Jascha (1901–87), Russian-American violin virtuoso, 64

Heinlein, Robert (1907–88), American author of science fiction, 99

Heller, Joseph (1923–99), American novelist, best known for *Catch-22*, 44, 234

Hemingway, Ernest (1899–1961), American author, winner of Nobel Prize in Literature, 124, 192

Heraclitus, 25, 69, 195, 209, 291

Herodotus, 38, 58, 140, 158, 173, 174, 193, 203, 280, 291

Herrick, Robert (ca. 1590–1674), British Cavalier poet, 240

Hesiod, 52, 55, 101, 138, 181, 185, 207, 260, 292

Hetfield, James (1963–), cofounder of heavy metal band Metallica, 40

Hightower, Jim (1943–), Texan activist, author, and politician, 20

Hippocrates, 62, 292

Hippolytus, 209, 292

Homer, 3, 66, 67, 101, 172, 187, 218, 230, 235, 246, 292

Horace, 3, 64, 68, 71, 81, 91, 92, 93, 116, 117, 122, 127, 145, 153, 161, 168, 175, 180, 183, 198, 200, 206, 207, 218, 219, 223, 237, 239, 244, 259, 261, 262, 263, 269, 292–93, 308

Printed and bound by PG in the USA

USA2019PGIL